Midland Castles

by Mike Salter

The history, fortifications and remains
of seventy six castles in the western Midlands,
with photographs, old engravings and scale plans.

Quercus

****
Quercus
John Roberts
8 Hillside Close, Bartley Green
Birmingham B32 4LT
****

Midland Castles

by Mike Salter

ISBN 1 898136 04 1

First Published 1993

Old print of Caverswall Castle

CONTENTS

ACKNOWLEDGEMENTS

The old prints in this book are reproduced from originals in the collection of the author, who also took all the black and white photographs and prepared the plans and drawings mostly from his own field surveys between 1969 and 1993.

Max Barfield provided word processor facilities, checked the text, and did the driving for some of the more recent field visits.

John Roberts took the cover photograph and acted as editor.

Marc Vyvyan-Jones drew the cartoon of Mike Salter which appears below.

ABOUT THE AUTHOR

Mike Salter is 40 and was born and brought up in Wolverhampton. Since 1990 he has lived in a cottage on the west side of the Malvern Hills. Mike spent periods in the Civil Service and with British Steel but has been a full time writer and publisher of books about medieval castles and parish churches in England, Wales, Scotland and Ireland since 1988. This book is his eighteenth gazetteer, the first one being Discovering Scottish Castles published by Shire in 1985. Mike has been interested in castles since he was about 10 and began to make his own measured drawings of them in the late 1960s. He now has a huge collection of photographs, brass rubbings and self-drawn plans from which the illustrations in his books are taken. Many of his favourite castles are in Scotland and Ireland, some of them being no bigger, although more massive, than his own cottage and court with a loopholed wall and small turreted gatehouse. Mike's other interests include folk music, morris dancing and model railways. He also plays a variety of percussion instruments.

MAP OF MIDLAND CASTLES

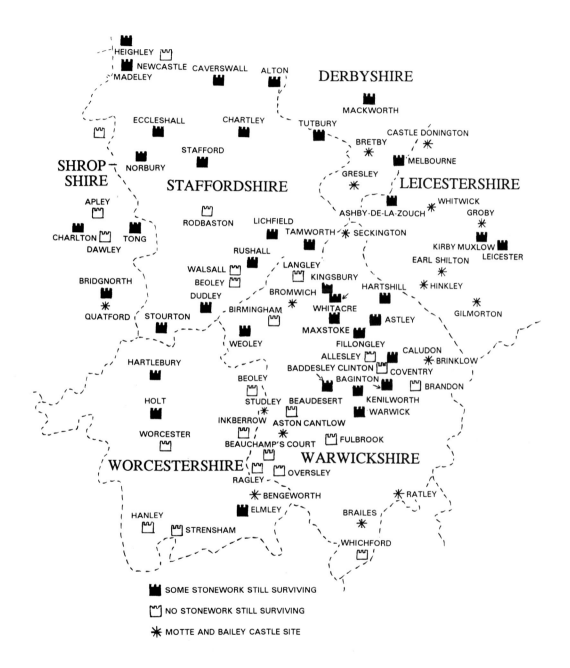

HEIGHLEY

NEWCASTLE   CAVERSWALL   ALTON   DERBYSHIRE

MADELEY

MACKWORTH

ECCLESHALL   CHARTLEY   TUTBURY   CASTLE DONINGTON

BRETBY

STAFFORD   MELBOURNE

NORBURY   GRESLEY   LEICESTERSHIRE

SHROP-   STAFFORDSHIRE

SHIRE

APLEY   ASHBY-DE-LA-ZOUCH   WHITWICK   GROBY

RODBASTON   LICHFIELD

CHARLTON   TONG   TAMWORTH   SECKINGTON

DAWLEY   KIRBY MUXLOW   LEICESTER

RUSHALL   EARL SHILTON

BRIDGNORTH   WALSALL   LANGLEY

BEOLEY   KINGSBURY   HARTSHILL   HINKLEY

DUDLEY   BROMWICH   GILMORTON

QUATFORD   STOURTON   BIRMINGHAM   WHITACRE   ASTLEY

MAXSTOKE

HARTLEBURY   WEOLEY   FILLONGLEY

ALLESLEY   CALUDON

BADDESLEY CLINTON   COVENTRY   BRINKLOW

BEOLEY   BAGINTON   BRANDON

HOLT   STUDLEY   BEAUDESERT   KENILWORTH

INKBERROW   ASTON CANTLOW   WARWICK

WORCESTER   BEAUCHAMP'S COURT   FULBROOK

WORCESTERSHIRE   WARWICKSHIRE

RAGLEY   OVERSLEY

BENGEWORTH   RATLEY

HANLEY   ELMLEY   BRAILES

STRENSHAM   WHICHFORD

SOME STONEWORK STILL SURVIVING

NO STONEWORK STILL SURVIVING

MOTTE AND BAILEY CASTLE SITE

5

CASTLES LIST AND REFERENCES

After each castle name appears the pre 1974 county, the O.S. grid reference, and the principal source(s) of information. The abbreviations are explained below.

Alton (Staffs) SK 073425 *B.O.E. p55-60, Renn p352, V.C.H. 1 p350*
Allesley (Warks) SP 304804 *V.C.H. 6 p3*
Apley (Salop) SJ 656132 *B.O.E. p60*
Ashby de la Zouch (Leics) SK 361167 *Eng Her Guide Book*
Astley (Warks) SP 313894) *V.C.H. 6 p15-18*
Aston Cantlow (Warks) SP 137600 *V.C.H. 3 p36*
Audley (Staffs) SJ 799511 *T.N.S.F.C. XLIX p92-6*
Baginton (Warks) SP 342747 *V.C.H. 6 p22-23*
Beauchamps' Court (Warks) SP 085586 *V.C.H. 3 p15-16*
Beaudesert (Warks) SP 155662 *V.C.H. 3 p45-46*
Bengeworth (Worcs) SP 041437 *V.C.H. 2 p398-9*
Beoley (Worcs) SP 066694 *V.C.H. 4 p15 & 432*
Bescot (Staffs) SP 998967 *V.C.H. 7 p171-2*
Birmingham (Warks) SP 074865 *T.B.W.A.S. 89 1978-9, V.C.H. 7*
Brailes (Warks) SP 308401 *V.C.H. 5 p18*
Brandon (Warks) SP 408759 *V.C.H. 6 p273-276*
Bretby (Derbys) SK 293231 *V.C.H. 1 p378-9*
Bridgnorth (Salop) SO 717927 *V.C.H.*
Brinklow (Warks) SP 439797 *V.C.H. 1 p360-2 6 p42*
Bromwich (Warks) SP 143901 *V.C.H. 4 p44*
Caludon (Warks) SP 374802 *V.C.H. 8 p121*
Castle Donington (Leics) SK 448276 *V.C.H. 1, D.C.E.W p102*
Caverswall (Staffs) SJ 951428 *C.Life XXIX 1911 p886-95, T.N.S.F.C 1937-8*
Chartley (Staffs) SK 010285 *V.C.H.*
Cheswardine (Salop) SJ 719301 *V.C.H.*
Coventry (Warks) SP 336788 *V.C.H. 8 p118*
Dawley (Salop) SJ 687063 *L. Guide p113*
Dudley (Staffs) SO 946907 *Official Guide Book, Archeological Journal LXXXI*
Earl Shilton (Leics) SP 471982 *V.C.H. p258*
Eccleshall (Staffs) SJ 828296 *B.O.E. p126, Renn p182, V.C.H. 1 p370*
Elmley (Worcs) SO 989403 *V.C.H. 3 p340 4 p431*
Fillongley (Warks) SP 280087 & 285877 *V.C.H. 1 p375 4 p69-71*
Fulbrook (Warks) SP 252607 *V.C.H. 5 p92-3*
Gilmorton (Leics) SP 570878 *V.C.H. 1 p258*
Gresley (Derbys) SK 274179 *V.C.H. 1 p379*
Groby (Leics) SK 524076 *V.C.H. 1 p258-9*
Hanley (Worcs) SO 838414 *V.C.H. 4 p93-96 431*
Hartlebury (Worcs) SO 836713 *Guide Leaflet, V.C.H. 3 p381-4*
Hartshill (Warks) SP 325944 *V.C.H. 4 p131-2*
Heighley (Staffs) SJ 733467 *V.C.H. 1 p351*
Hinckley (Leics) SP 428935 *V.C.H. 1 p257*
Holt (Worcs) SO 831626 *V.C.H. 3 p401-5*
Inkberrow (Worcs) SP 017573 *V.C.H. 3 p421-3*
Kenilworth (Warks) SP 279723 *Eng Her Guide Book, V.C.H.*

Kingsbury (Warks) SP 214964 *V.C.H. 4 p100-102*
Kirby Muxloe (Leics) (SK 524046) *Eng Her Guide Book*
Langley (Warks) SP 152956 *T.B.W.A.S. 1947-8 LXVII*
Leicester (Leics) SK 582041 *V.C.H. 1 p260-1 4 p344-47*
Lichfield (Staffs) SK 116097 *V.C.H. 1 & 14, T.S.S.A.S. XXV*
Mackworth (Derbys) SK 318377 *B.O.E.*
Madeley (Staffs) SJ 773423 *V.C.H. 1*
Maxstoke (Warks) SP 224892 *V.C.H. 4 p132-6*
Melbourne (Derbys) SK 389252 *D.C.E.W.*
Newcastle-Under-Lyme (Staffs) SJ 844459 *Pape, V.C.H. 1*
Norbury (Staffs) SJ 797233 *V.C.H. 4 p155-6*
Oversley (Warks) SP 099553 *V.C.H. 3 p29*
Ragley (Warks) SP 072555 *V.C.H. 3 p29*
Ratley (Warks) SP 381473 *V.C.H. 1*
Rodbaston (Staffs) SJ 921124 *V.C.H. 5 p120-2*
Rushall (Staffs) SP 026998 *T.S.S.A.S. 1981-2 XXIII p79-88*
Seckington (Warks) SK 258075 *V.C.H. 1 p390-2 4 p198*
Stafford (Staffs) SJ 902222 *Renn p315, W.S.A.S. VIII p6-22, V.C.H 1 & 6*
Stourton (Staffs) SO 859849 *V.C.H. 1 p369 20 p130-2*
Strensham (Worcs) SO 904405 *V.C.H. 4 431-433*
Studley (Warks) SP 082638 *V.C.H. 3 p180*
Tamworth (Staffs) SK 207039 *B.O.E. p277, Guide Book, Renn p319, V.C.H. 1*
Tong (Salop) SJ 292069 *Excavation report obtained by author on site in 1978*
Tutbury (Staffs) SK 209291 *Guide Book by Sir Robert Somerville 1964, V.C.H.*
Walsall (Staffs) SP 001984 *T.S.S.A.S. 1974-5 XVI p19-53, V.C.H.*
Warwick (Warks) SP 284646 *Guide Book. V.C.H. p452-60*
Weoley (Warks) SP 022827 *Med Arch 1962, T.B.W.A.S. 28 1902 78 1962*
Whichford (Warks) SP 308346 *V.C.H. 5 p144*
Whitacre (Warks) SP 242937 *V.C.H. 4 251*
Whitwick (Leics) SK 436162 *V.C.H. 1 261-2, D.C.E.W. p103*
Wolseley (Staffs) SK 034204 *Little is available apart from an old print.*
Worcester (Worcs) SO 849547 *V.C.H. 4 p390-91*

B.O.E.	Buildings of England series, one volume for each county, mostly by N.Pevsner, 1951-1974
C.Life	Country Life Magazine
D.C.E.W.	Discovering Castles in England and Wales, John Kinross 1973
Eng Her	English Heritage/Dept of Environment/Ministry of Works pamphlets
L. Guide	Shropshire volume of Little Guides series, J.E. Auden, 1912
Med. Arch.	Medieval Archaeology
Pape	Medieval Newcastle-Under-Lyme, T.Pape, 1928
Renn	Norman Castles in Britain, Derek Renn, 1968
S. Shaw	The History and Antiqities of Staffordshire, Stebbing Shaw, 1798
T.B.W.A.S.	Transactions of Birmingham and West Midlands Archaeological Society
T.N.S.F.C.	Transactions of North Staffordshire Field Club
T.S.S.A.S.	Transactions of South Staffordshire Archaeological & Historical Society
V.C.H.	Victoria County Histories, several vols for each county.
W.S.A.S.	William Salt Archaeological Society Transactions

INTRODUCTION

Books about the history and architecture of castles depend upon records and physical remains. A few castles like Warwick still essentially retain their medieval buildings, if in a somewhat repaired and modernised form. Others like Kenilworth and Dudley form noble ruins. Some castles now show no more than a single modest fragment, and several have vanished entirely. Hanley, Newcastle and Tong have well-documented histories, although hardly anything survives above ground. Where there is a short gazetteer entry this is because little or nothing remains, the site has not been excavated, and few records have survived.

Technical terms like "barbican" and "ringwork" are explained in the Glossary at the back of the book. The few legal expressions can be understood if you appreciate that from 1066 all land beloned to the Crown who let it in large tracts to Tenants in Chief. They in turn sublet portions to tenants who might in turn sublet. Land sometimes returned to the Crown because of the lack of an heir or the forfeiture of tenants who rebelled or plotted against the government. In these cases the estate might remain royal or be granted to another tenant.

When the Normans invaded England in 1066 they brought with them the concept of a new type of fortress called a castle which was different both in appearance and purpose from the communal forts of Roman and Saxon times. The first castles in the Midlands were those built by William the Conqueror at Warwick in 1068 and Stafford in 1070, but the majority of the new castles were privately owned fortress-residences of his barons and their knights. Under the feudal system then introduced each rank held land from that immediately above it in return for military service which included garrison duty in the new castles. It was by building such structures which became symbols of lordly rank that the new regime maintained its position of dominance over the Saxon populace.

Of the dozen or so castles which existed in the area under discussion by the year 1100 none of them originally had defences or domestic buildings of mortared stone. Rapid construction was required and the large numbers of skilled masons which would be required were simply not available because the Saxons generally used wood for buildings. So the new castles took the form of earthworks, which could be created with unskilled slave labour, surmounted by stockades and timber buildings with thatched roofs. The layout and size of each castle varies considerably according to the terrain chosen and the resources available, but a common layout comprised a mound called a motte with an adjoining court called a bailey defended by a rampart. Earth was piled up from surrounding ditches which were normally dry. The bailey contained a hall and chapel and an array of buildings used as workshops and for storing agricultural produce, stock, tools and munitions. The lord and his family when they were in residence (the greater lords had several castles in addition to undefended manor houses) lived in a wooden tower or house within a tiny palisaded court upon the mound summit which was reached from the bailey by a wooden ramp and perhaps a drawbridge.

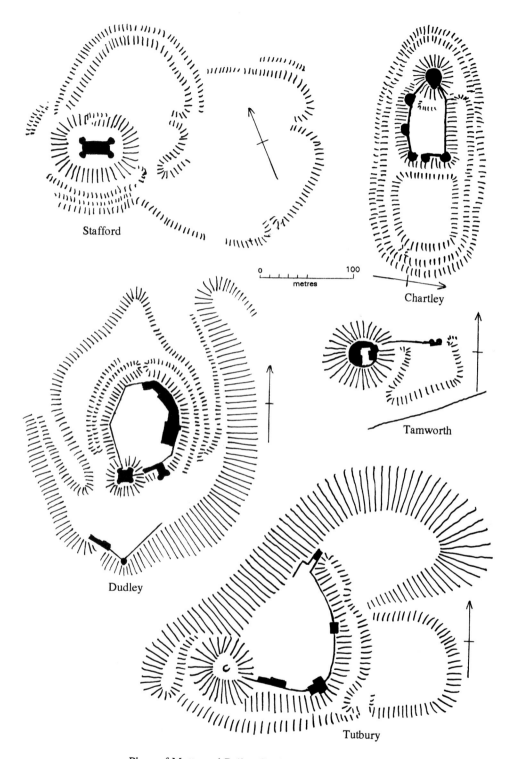

Stafford

Chartley

0 100
metres

Tamworth

Dudley

Tutbury

Plans of Motte and Bailey Castles in Staffordshire

Castles played a vital part in the conflicts between King Stephen (1135-54) and the supporters of Henry I's daughter Maud. Sieges were much more common than pitched battles and some of the castles proved quite hard to take by simple force of arms. Garrisons often had to be starved into submission which tied up a large blockading force for a very long time during which an army might come to the relief of those within. Many new castles were built in the years before and during the conflict, some of which were of an alternative type where a ringwork or small and well defended inner bailey took the place of the motte, as at Beaudesert. The low lying castles of Kenilworth and Brandon were given elaborate water defences created by blocking and diverting streams. In 1148 the Earls of Leicester and Chester made a treaty limiting the number of castles allowed between Leicester, Coventry, and Tamworth.

Wood continued to be the primary building material until the end of the 12th century when some of the more important castles such as Warwick, Tutbury, Coventry, Dudley, and Kenilworth began to be rebuilt in stone. Earlier stone defences survive only at Tamworth where the thick section of bailey wall forming a causeway up the motte may be of c1100-25, whilst the keep may be of c1125-40. It takes the form of a polygonal shell wall replacing the motte stockade and having a small projecting tower commanding the entrance. Similar shell walls at Warwick and Tutbury were not built until the 1180s or later. Excavations have revealed traces of a crude early gate tower at Ratley. At Leicester a large chapel of the 1120s and an aisled hall of c1150 with wooden arcades survive in a much altered state. Alton Castle, being built on virgin rock, seems to have been of stone as first built in the 1180s.

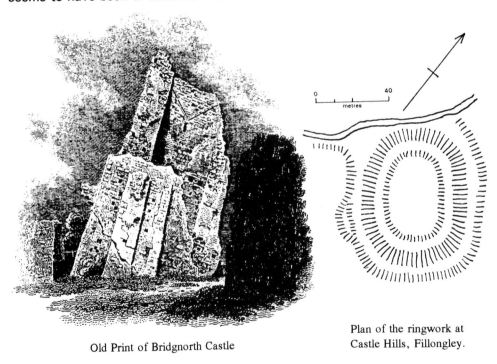

Old Print of Bridgnorth Castle

Plan of the ringwork at Castle Hills, Fillongley.

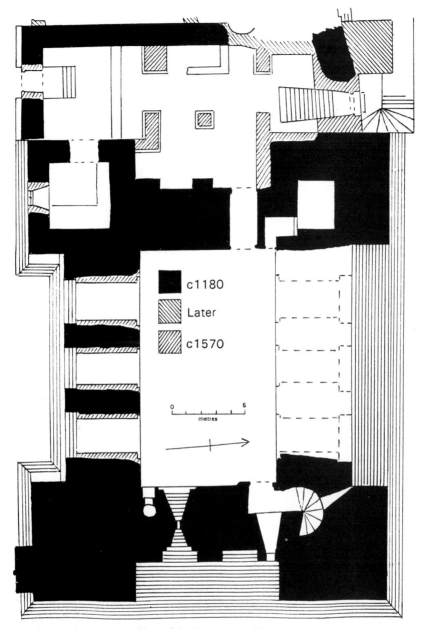

c1180

Later

c1570

0   5
metres

Plan of the keep at Kenilworth

Part of a keep built by Henry II in c1166-74 remains at Bridgnorth. It contained a dark storage basement, a hall reached by steps in a forebuilding, and a private room above. Very little remains of similar keeps at Stafford and Elmley, and nothing of that at Newcastle, but most of the huge two storey keep built by Henry II in the 1180s at Kenilworth survives. This keep and those of Newcastle and Elmley were accompanied by bailey walls built by the end of the 12th century.

11

In the early years of the 13th century King John greatly strengthened Kenilworth by adding an outer bailey and improving the water defences. The weakest side has flanking towers at either end, one round and the other octagonal on a square base. Further improvements continued to be made and the castle was so strong that it was able to hold out against the entire military might of the kingdom in 1266 until starved until submission. Brandon has traces of an early 13th century keep with some resemblance to that at Kenilworth. The Earl of Chester's castle of the 1220s at Chartley heralds a new type of fortress using ideas developed by the Crusaders. It has a modestly sized rectangular court with several large and massive round towers providing all round flanking fire by means of tall cross shaped arrow loops. Two towers were placed close together with the gateway between them. The castle was built on earlier earthworks and has a large round keep on a motte. Another round tower keep of about the same period once stood at Tutbury, but was placed on flat ground better able to take the weight rather than the motte. These towers were probably of three storeys, with a hall above a storage basement and the lord's private room on top but little remains of them, and nothing of other courts with round towers at Stourton and Beaudesert. Nor has anything survived of King John's hunting seat at Hanley. Only footings remain of a castle at Heighley which seems to have had a twin towered gatehouse like Chartley, although its cliff top location and rock-cut ditch made it more akin to another of the Earl of Chester's castles not far away at Beeston.

Lunn's Tower, Kenilworth Castle

The building of private fortifications was controlled by the Crown which issued to those in favour and thought to be trustworthy with licences to crenellate. It was on these terms that the Bishop of Worcester fortified his manor house of Hartlebury c1270, and the Bishop of Lichfield did likewise with his country seat at Eccleshall and his own cathedral close at Lichfield. All these were rectangular enclosures with twin towered gatehouses and polygonal corner towers. A fourth example of this plan survives in a more complete state at Caverswall. The courts at Weoley and Astley were more irregularly shaped and had rectangular towers. All these sites were protected by wide water filled moats. The destroyed outer bailey defences at Tong with round corner towers and a square gatehouse may also have been of this period.

Many crenellation licences were granted during the first half of the 14th century, especially during the lawless years of Edward II's reign when many local gentry were keen to protect themselves from overmighty neighbours such as Sir John de Somery, Lord of Dudley. Dawley has vanished and little remains other than the moats at Apley, Beauchamps' Court, Charlton and Whichford, but there are fragments of curtain walls at Hartshill, Melbourne, and Kingsbury, the latter having one octagonal tower and evidence of another, plus a square gatehouse. Low walls with three square towers remain with a moat at Whitacre. More impressive are the bailey walls, gatehouse, solar block, and the tower house with round corner towers on the mound at Dudley, and there is also a gatehouse at Tutbury. Maxstoke has a very complete circuit of curtain walls of the 1340s with octagonal corner towers, a wet moat, and a gatehouse with octagonal turrets facing the field. The domestic buildings were rebuilt in the 15th and 16th centuries but originally abutted against the three sides away from the gateway.

Maxstoke Castle

Gatehouse, Warwick Castle

Warwick and Kenilworth have important and impressive remains of the later 14th century displaying to all the high rank and great power of their builders. The Beauchamps built a fine show front at one end of the bailey at Warwick with a gatehouse and barbican in the middle and lofty towers at either end. One is twelve sided, the other has a unique tri-lobed plan, and both have parapets with machicolations or murder holes commanding the base of the walls and through which missiles could be dropped or fired. The apartments of the same period have been mostly rebuilt except for the vaulted cellars. Extensive vaulted cellars were also a feature of the palatial new hall and apartments built by John of Gaunt at Kenilworth. There are tower-like wings at either end of the hall with octagonal corner turrets and delightful bay windows faced the court.

There are slight remains on the mound at Stafford of a very large tower house with octagonal corner towers begun in the 1340s, while Ashby de la Zouch has a large and massive rectangular tower which contained a huge kitchen. Near Coventry are the castles of Caludon which has part of one wall of a hall within a moat and Baginton with the lower part of a large self contained block in which was a hall and chamber side by side over a series of vaulted cellars. A tower remaining at Holt was probably one of four at the corners of a hall block with a similar layout but less massive walling than the tower house at Stafford. The fragment at Madeley may be of either a roofed building or a courtyard.

From the early 15th century are two modest gatehouses and some walling at Leicester and most of the curtain wall with two rectangular self contained towers at Tutbury. Both castles were then in the hands of the Crown. No details are known of the new castle at Fulbrook except that it was built of brick. Astley, Hartlebury and Tamworth have hall blocks of the mid 15th century. Castles only played a minor role in the struggles known as the Wars Of The Roses, but of some considerable interest are the works of leading Yorkists in the 1470s and 80s as part of their attempt to consolidate their uncertain political position. Lord Hastings rebuilt his manor houses of Ashby de la Zouch and Kirby Muxloe as castles, Ashby gaining a fine stone built tower house and Kirby a quadrangular court of brick with a wet moat, square corner towers and a gatehouse consisting of a rectangular block with octagonal turrets. Richard III's tower house at Warwick has the same plan as the Kirby Muxloe gatehouse also left unfinished because of the builder's sudden violent death. Both these buildings are furnished with gunports for cannon. Artillery was now increasingly important and was fast making defences based on high stone curtain walls obsolete, and these works are the last of their type in the area. Nothing is known for certain of the layout at Wolseley and only a gateway of 1495 remains at Mackworth.

Richard III's incomplete tower at Warwick.

On the whole the rooms inside medieval buildings were dark, cold, and rather bare. Until at least the 14th century glass was uncommon and windows were closed with shutters in bad weather. Wide openings within reach of the ground would usually have iron stanchions. Fireplaces were sometimes provided in the walls but the main hall might have a central fireplace with the smoke escaping through a louvre in the roof. Window embrasures sometimes have stone seats but movable furnishings were sparse and simple. Great lords with castles and manor houses scattered across the country tended to circulate so as to consume agricultural produce in situ. Their servants and portable furnishings went with them, only caretakers being left to maintain a castle except when a garrison was required in times of unrest. Often the castles were left to decay until such time as they again became favoured as a residence or required as a fortress. Surveyors' lists of serious structural defects to castles, especially those in royal hands, are very common because to keep the defences, apartments, grounds, and domestic and military equipment at all of them in a permanent pristine state was far too expensive even for the richest of lords.

The internal walls of the rooms reserved for the lord and his family were often plastered and painted with allegorical or biblical scenes or floral or geometrical patterns. Wall hangings with the same motifs became increasing fashionable as time went on but were very expensive. External walls also might be plastered unless they were faced with finely cut stone. It is not often realised that many of the buildings were whitewashed both inside and out. Usually only scanty traces of this survive today, so that even fairly complete walls may have a drastically changed appearance. By the 14th century towers and lean-to ranges were used to contain private rooms with fireplaces and latrines for lesser household members, but in earlier times there was hardly any privacy in a castle. Regardless of rank, even lords and ladies often had servants sleeping on couches in their private rooms, although the lordly bed would be screened off. Other members of the household bedded down in the main hall or anywhere else where a modicum of warmth and privacy might be found. Those who enjoyed the luxury of a proper bed would normally have to share it with several others of the same sex. Few people would have more than one or two sets of clothes, spare sets being kept in chests rather than in wardrobes. Other chests were used to store eating and drinking utensils and valuables of all kinds.

The domestic buildings in the bailey at Dudley.

Scattered across the Midlands are numerous rectangular or nearly rectangular moated enclosures marking the sites of former manor houses. They mostly date from the 13th and 14th centuries and are particular common in the Forest of Arden where they seem to be associated with the reclamation of waste land. Many moats only had a hedge or fence on the inner side of the ditch with the house inside partly or wholly built of perishable materials like timber or wattle and daub with thatched roofs. But a few moats had modest stone walls on the inner edge of the moat or ranges of buildings, without towers or battlements, set around a central court. Baddesley Clinton has quite a well preserved house of this sort with a pair of gunports, perhaps ornamental rather than functional, in the porch. It is not easy to say which of these sites should be regarded as being seriously fortified and thus classifiable as castles. Medieval documents are notoriously ambiguous as to what was then regarded as a house or castle, buildings sometimes being first described as one and then later as another. Nor can we be sure if high stone walls and towers were actually built in some cases despite records of crenellation licences being issued, and in one instance at Walsall materials being stockpiled ready. A building like Rushall Hall is hard to classify. It is never described as a castle yet it has a high but thin curtain wall, which is not a normal feature of an unfortified manor house, and a later gatehouse. With the aid of additional earthworks it put up a fierce resistance to attack in the Civil War.

Baddesley Clinton Hall

Old print of the former moated mansion at Himley, near Dudley.

A water filled ditch around a manor house was not necessarily military in purpose and did not require a royal licence. It was a symbol of rank as only manorial lords and a few high born parochial clergy could afford to hire or call upon the sort of labour force needed to create a moat. It formed a useful barrier if the only access to the central platform was by means of a drawbridge as was normally the case. The combination of water and mud at the bottom would effectively exclude not just small raiding parties but vagrants, malefactors and wild animals, and would keep in the domestic animals, servants and children. Moats were appreciated as scenic features and helped to drain boggy land, to flush latrines, and to provide a habitat for fish and water fowl which formed in the medieval period a much more important part of the normal daily diet than they generally do today.

Many of the castles have or had domestic ranges of the 16th and 17th centuries, but quite a number had already been abandoned and material was being removed from them, legally or otherwise. Little remains of Henry VIII's works at Warwick and Kenilworth but there are impressive ruins of John Dudley's hall and apartments at Dudley and of a block built by the Earl of Leicester at Kenilworth to accommodate Queen Elizabeth I when she came to stay. A block was also built at Warwick for the same reason, and another was erected at Tutbury for the captive Mary, Queen of Scots. Kenilworth also has a fine late 16th century stable block and a gatehouse with octagonal corner turrets whilst the garden has recently been restored to its original form. The garden at Ashby de la Zouch had ornamental ponds and a pair of summer houses on the outer wall. The hall block at Astley was remodelled probably at the end of the 16th century. and similar work was carried out at Warwick c1610-20. At the same time a lodge was built over the gateway at Tamworth and the hall given a new porch and staircase turret, whilst at Caverswall a new house was built within the defences and the towers remodelled. Tutbury has a few traces of a new hall built in the 1630s and also once had a spacious garden created within an outer bailey.

Several of the castles played an active part in the Civil War of 1642-6, being hastily repaired and strengthened by their owners. Warwick and Maxstoke were held by the Parliamentarian Lord Brooke who was killed during an attack on Lichfield, but most of the other castles were held for the King and were gradually reduced one by one as the war turned against him. They were subsequently made untenable as fortresses by breaches being opened in the walls, battlements being knocked off, portcullises and doors removed, and sometimes almost total destruction with gunpowder and undermining. Towers at Dudley, Kenilworth, and Tutbury all had their most exposed walls destroyed to the footings, the keep of Bridgnorth was reduced to a leaning fragment, and little was left at Stafford. Luckily an order for slighting at Maxstoke was not carried out.

Partial or complete replacement in the late 17th and 18th centuries of domestic buildings wrecked in the Civil War allowed Eccleshall, Hartlebury, Stourton and Tutbury to continue in use as residences, although Tutbury only housed a tenant farmer. Domestic buildings which are now derelict at Astley and Kingsbury were habitable earlier this century. Caverswall, Holt, Maxstoke, Warwick, the hall at Leicester and the keep at Tamworth also remain fully roofed. Alton was mostly rebuilt in the 19th century leaving only a few ruined parts. From the late 18th century onwards the more notable ruins began to attract visitors and inspire novelists like Sir Walter Scott. From the early 20th century onwards custody and maintenance of some of the ruins was taken over by the state. Ashby, Kirby, and Kenilworth are now maintained by English Heritage and Bridgnorth, Caludon, Dudley, Stafford, Tamworth and Weoley are looked after by local councils. The Duchy of Lancaster maintains Tutbury while Warwick has fairly recently passed into the care of the tourist exhibition firm Madame Tussauds, and Eccleshall is also occasionally open to the public.

GAZETTEER OF MIDLAND CASTLES

Alton *Near Alton Towers, 5 miles north of Uttoxeter.*

At the north end of the village of Alton, on a rock rising spectacularly above the ravine of the River Churnet, and within sight of Alton Towers, are the last remnants of a castle built c1170 by Bertram de Verdon. He died while on crusade with Richard I in the Holy Land in the 1190s. His castle comprised an oval court about 90m long by 40m wide with a rock-cut ditch isolating it from the level ground to the south and east. Stone from the ditch was used to build a curtain wall about 2m thick on the inner edge. The entrance was in the middle of a straight length of wall flanked at the west end by a square ashlar-faced tower which still partly remains, together with fragments of the curtain. The upper storey of the tower, with a crossloop and chamfered corners, is of c1300, and the base of a second tower of that date lies near the south-west corner.

Theobald de Verdon is said to have rebuilt the domestic buildings in the early 14th century. Nothing remains of them, but the splendid hall and solar blocks at the similarly sited castle of Ludlow in Shropshire in which the de Verdons then had a half share, give an indication of what may once have stood above the cliff edge at Alton. On Theobald's death in 1316 Alton passed by marriage to the Furnivals, and in 1406 it again passed by marriage to John Talbot, who assumed the title Lord Furnival, and was created Earl of Shrewsbury in 1442 by Henry VI for his services in France. He probably restored the castle for occasional use.

Old Print of Alton Castle

20

Alton Castle

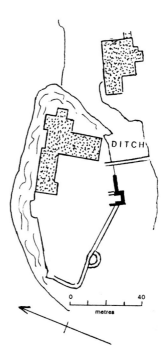

Plan of Alton Castle

George Talbot, 6th Earl of Shrewsbury, was husband of the famed Bess of Hardwick, and for a while had custody of the captive Mary, Queen of Scots. Alton Castle was held for King Charles in the Civil War and was later rendered untenable by order of Parliament. In 1787 Charles Talbot, 15th Earl, began to develop an outlying lodge and its grounds on a much more spacious site on the other side of the river. The work continued during the 19th century to create the huge mansion, now ruined, called Alton Towers. In 1847 the then Earl or a kinsman commissioned Pugin to build a romantic mock castle on the site of the former domestic buildings of the original castle, parts of which were cleared away to make room for the new works. Seven years earlier Pugin had masterminded the building of a Catholic college immediately south of the ditch, and the two form a fine grouping. The castle is not open to the public.

Allesley   *North-west of Coventry city centre.*

The Hastings family held the manor of Allesley from the mid 13th century until 1399, when it passed to Lord Bergavenny, a member of the Beauchamp family. The manor house was replaced in the early 14th century by a fortified building of which there are no remains and about which nothing is known. It was merely a site by the 1580s but traces of the moat were still visible in the 19th century.

Apley   *2 miles north of Wellington.*

In 1309 John de Charlton gained the castle and lordship of Powis by marriage, and in 1317 Edward II licensed him to crenellate his original chief seat at Charlton, near Wellington. He then built there a rectangular walled court surrounded by a wet moat and containing ranges of domestic buildings. In 1327 the young Edward III authorised Alan de Charlton to build two further fortified houses of this type at Withyford and Apley. Of the latter there remain only a pool which is relic of the former moat, and two doorways now reset on the north-west side of a stable block of c1600 which itself is the only relic of a new house built for Thomas Hanmer at a cost of £6,000. He garrisoned it for the King in 1643 and when it was eventually captured plunder worth £1,500 was removed and the building dismantled. The stable block was remodelled in the 18th century when another house was built, also now demolished.

Hastings Tower, Ashby-De-La-Zouch Castle

22

Ashby de la Zouch *Beside Ashby town centre.*

The manor of Ashby had a simple unfortified manor house, originally of timber, which was rebuilt in stone either by Philip de Beaumont in the 1150s, or his successor Alan la Zouch, a Breton nobleman, in the 1160s. The walls of the original solar block and parts of the hall remain from this period. The piers in the hall are later but must have replaced timber posts as the width of the building suggests that it always had aisles. The Zouch family were of some importance in the 13th century, having manors in Shropshire and Devon as well as Leicestershire, and holding such major offices as Constable of the Tower of London, Justice of Chester, and Justice of Ireland.

When the Zouch senior line failed in 1314 Ashby passed to a member of a junior branch of the Mortimer family, Sir William, of Richard's Castle in Herefordshire. He assumed the Zouch surname and was created Baron Zouch of Ashby in 1323. An inquisition after the death of Alan la Zouch, William's son, in 1347 suggests that the new solar block to the east was then under construction, and the hall, described as ruinous, was about to be rebuilt. Shortly after this the Kitchen Tower was added to the west of the original solar block, now relegated to a service wing. This tower is a huge structure nearly 20m long by 13.5m wide externally. The west wall facing the field was as much as 3m thick. Despite this, the arrangements of the building do not suggest a defensive structure, and there is no evidence that the manor house was made properly defensible before the 1470s. The tower contained several living rooms on a single storey above a most impressive kitchen at ground level with many fireplaces, ovens, a rib vault 9m high, and no less than three entrances.

Ashby-De-La-Zouche Castle

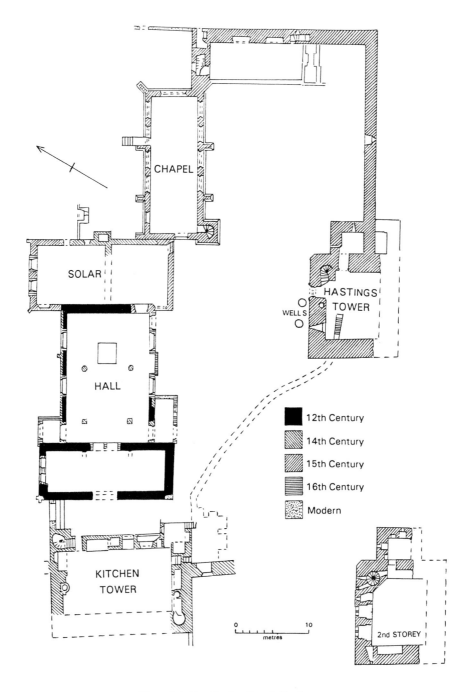

CHAPEL

SOLAR

HALL

HASTINGS
TOWER

WELL S

KITCHEN
TOWER

■ 12th Century

▨ 14th Century

▨ 15th Century

▤ 16th Century

⊡ Modern

2nd STOREY

0   10
metres

Plan of Ashby-De-La-Zouch Castle

The male line failed again with Hugh la Zouch's death in 1399 and Ashby passed through the hands of several families during the early 15th century. The only work of this period to the fabric was a northward extension of the new solar block. The manor reverted to the Crown in 1461 after James Butler, Earl of Ormonde, was executed following capture at the battle of Towton by the forces of the victorious Duke of York, who then assumed the throne as Edward IV. In 1464 King Edward gave Ashby to his Chamberlain, William, Lord Hastings, whose original seat was a then unfortified manor house at Kirby Muxloe (see page 58). Lord Hastings added a chapel beyond the south-east corner of the new solar block and then began to lay out a court to the south of the chapel, with offices and apartments in ranges leaning against a thick new curtain wall.

In April 1474 Edward IV granted Lord Hastings a licence for the fortification of his manor houses at Ashby, Kirby Muxloe, and Bagworth. At Ashby it seems that whatever curtain walls were still required to securely enclose courts on either side of the older domestic buildings were then provided. An impressive new tower house to provide Lord Hastings with secure private accommodation was hastily added in the middle of the outer south wall, away from the older buildings, except for the south-west corner of the new court south of the chapel. The tower has a main block 14m by 12m over walls up to 2.5m thick, and was entered at ground level by a doorway closed by a portcullis. The basement, which has a well, and the kitchen above were vaulted, then there was a hall or audience room, and above that the private chamber. A wing on the east side contained six stories of smaller private rooms over a strongroom. There is a small but fine vaulted oriel opening off the hall. It is contained within the base of one of the octagonal corner turrets rising from the upper parts of the tower, which now rises about 22m, but which originally had machicolated parapets of which only the corbels remain giving a total height of about 25m.

Lord Hastings was executed by the Duke of Gloucester shortly after the latter assumed power as Richard III in 1483, but the Hastings family retained the estates and supported the Earl of Richmond, who as Henry VII visited Ashby in 1503. In 1529 Henry VIII created Lord Hastings' grandson Earl of Huntingdon. The third Earl was Lord President of the Council of the North under Elizabeth I and Ashby Castle was visited by the captive Mary, Queen of Scots in 1569 and 1586. During this period the hall was again remodelled, being given large new windows, north and south porches, and a mural fireplace to replace the former central hearth. A further development was the laying out of a wild garden called the "Wilderness" to the south with a brick enclosing wall having a two storey octagonal garden tower at the south-east corner, and an even more impressive three storey quatrefoil shaped tower at the south-west corner. Under James I, who visited Ashby in 1614 and 1617, the Earls lived at the castle in great state with a household as big as sixty eight people recorded in 1609. However, the cost of the lavish entertainments of the second royal visit, for which another apartment block is thought to have been hastily erected, strained the resources of the then Earl to the limit. Despite this there was another expensive royal visit in 1634 when Charles I and his Queen Henrietta Maria came to stay at Ashby.

The 6th Earl of Huntingdon, who succeeded in 1643, took no part in the Civil War but his younger brother Henry Hastings used the castle as a base for Royalist military operations throughout the east Midlands. He improved the defences and is said to have provided an underground passage out to the Mount House built in 1644 to accommodate Irish troops and act as an outwork. A still surviving passage connecting the Kitchen Tower to the Hastings' Tower, is likely to date from the same period as the latter tower, i.e. the 1470s. The castle was besieged by Parliamentary forces after the battle of Naseby but was regarded as too strong to storm. Starvation and plague eventually induced the garrison to surrender in February 1646. The castle was ordered to be made untenable although this was not carried out until 1649 when the south wall of the Hastings' Tower was undermined and blown up, thus reducing it to the foundations, and the west wall of the Kitchen Tower was similarly treated. The Hastings family subsequently lived at Donington Park, although a new house called Ashby Place was built near the castle in the 1720s, and S. and N. Buck's engraving of the castle in 1730 shows that the hall, solar, chapel, and other domestic buildings were then still roofed. Walter Scott's novel "Ivanhoe" published in 1819 revived public interest in the ruins which were taken into state guardianship in 1932. They are now administered by English Heritage.

Old Print of Ashby-De-La-Zouch Castle

26

Astley Castle

Astley   *4 miles south-west of Nuneaton*

It was probably Andrew de Astley who built a curtain wall around an oval platform 75m long by 57m wide in the middle of a square wet moat during Edward I's reign. After Andrew's father Thomas was killed fighting for Simon de Montfort at the battle of Evesham in 1265, Henry III gave the manor to Warine de Bassingburn, with a licence for a crenellated stone wall, but it appears to have been restored to the original family before any work could begin. Fragments of the wall survive, together with one tower 10m square now embedded in later apartments.

When the Astley male line failed in 1420 the castle passed to Reynald, Lord Grey of Ruthin. His descendants intermarried with the Staffords and built in the 15th century a new hall block. Queen Mary supposedly had the castle destroyed in 1554 after Lady Jane Grey's nine day reign, the latter's father, Henry, Duke of Stafford, then being owner. Mary gave Astley to Edward Chamberlain who seems to have rebuilt the domestic buildings. The castle was subsequently leased to various families until sold in the late 17th century to Sir Richard Newdigate. When the last of his male line failed in 1806 Astley went to the Parkers who then assumed the Newdigate name. The apartments, which contain some 15th century work, but are mostly of c1550-1620 with later additions and alterations, served as a hotel as recently as the late 1970s. They are now totally ruined and the castle has been abandoned and shut up.

Old print of Astley Castle

Aston Cantlow *7 miles south-east of Redditch.*

Only faint traces of a ringwork beside the River Alne remain of a castle which was the chief seat of the Cantilupe from the early 12th century until William Cantilupe obtained several other castles by marrying Eva de Braose in the 1240s.

Audley *6 miles north-west of Stoke-on-Trent.*

A natural hill north of the church was adapted by the Audley family in the 12th century to form a low motte 40m across on top. Excavations found a coin of 1272-1327 and some thin walling probably of the same period.

Baginton *2 miles south of Coventry city centre.*

The Herthills are said to have had a house here on the end of a ridge above the River Soar, but the castle was built by Sir William Bagot in the 1390s. Bagot was one of Richard II's unpopular money raisers but managed to survive his master's downfall in 1399. His heiress married Thomas Stafford who sold Baginton to the Earl of Warwick. It was later conveyed to the Dean and Chapter of St Mary's church at Warwick and later passed to the Gooderes and Bromleys. However, the castle seems to have been a ruin when Leland saw it c1540 and it may never have been properly completed, being just allowed to decay after Bagot's death.

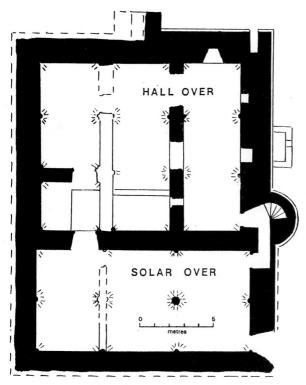

Plan of Baginton Castle

Baginton Castle

The castle comprised a court about 40m square probably originally with buildings on all sides although the only remains, heavily overgrown and nowhere more than 2m high, are of a small tower facing the river and a large self contained hall block facing the approach. The ashlar walling of the latter is up to 2m thick and has responds and piers for vaulting. The space below the hall measures 13.6m by 11m, and that below the private chamber alongside it 14.4m by 6.6m. A spiral stair in a round mid-wall turret led up to the hall, at which level was the entrance, probably by means of a drawbridge. It is unlikely that there was a third storey. The castle site lies on private ground and is not open to the public.

Beauchamps' Court *On the north side of Alcester.*

In 1340 Giles de Beauchamp obtained a licence from Edward III to crenellate his manor house near Alcester, and surround it with a wall of stone and lime. In the 1530s the house passed to Fulke Greville who rebuilt it using materials salvaged from Alcester Priory. After the Grevilles transferred their seat to Warwick in the early 17th century Beauchamps' Court was little used, and was left empty after William Greville died in 1653. Part of the house was demolished in 1667, probably to avoid hearth-tax. Only an overgrown moated platform now survives.

Beaudesert   *Near Henley-in-Arden, 8 miles south of Solihull*

In the early 12th century Thurstan de Montfort obtained part of the manor of Preston Bagot from Henry de Newburgh, Earl of Warwick. He named the new estate Beaudesert - beautiful wasteland - and built an oval ringwork with two outer baileys in line on a ridge south of where the village later grew up. A stone keep is thought to have been added before the end of the century, and Peter de Montfort, who was killed alongside his kinsman Simon, Earl of Leicester at the battle of Evesham in 1265, is said to have added a curtain wall with round flanking towers. On the death of Peter de Montfort in 1369 Beaudesert reverted to the Earl of Warwick. The hall porch was repaired in 1411 but the stonework had all been taken for building elsewhere by the end of the 16th century.

Bengeworth   *Close to Evesham town centre.*

It was probably Walter de Beauchamp who built a castle by the bridge over the River Severn during the lawless years of King Stephen's reign (1135-54). He was excommunicated for a raid on the neighbouring Abbey of Evesham. Abbot William de Andeville sent forces to occupy and destroy the castle and a cemetery was created on the site, although the Beauchamps did not officially surrender the site to the church until 1268. The moat was still partly visible a century ago.

Beoley   *3 miles north of Redditch.*

The site of the Beauchamps' house, accidentally burnt in 1303 and back in use as a court and grange in 1316, may be the strongly sited oval area 100m long by 85m wide with a surrounding ditch. Probably of 12th century origin, it is a promontory site commanding extensive views towards the south west.

Bescot   *1 mile south of Walsall.*

The last traces of moats which vanished c1970 belonged to the mansion built c1300 by William Hillary after he gained a considerable addition to his estate from his overlord Roger de Morteyn, Lord of Walsall. He was besieged there in 1311 by a party of fifty men led by Thomas le Rous. Bescot was held by the Mountford family for much of the 15th century. Sir Simon Mountford was attainted for treason in 1495, but his heirs recovered Bescot in 1534 and held it until the 1670s. It was taxed on no less than fourteen hearths in 1666. The house later passed to the Slaneys and was eventually demolished, a new house being built to the north-east of the moat, over which a bridge was built. This house was subsequently leased to tenants and was in turn demolished c1930.

Birmingham *Near St Martin's Church in the Bullring.*

In 1166 Peter de Birmingham was authorised to hold a market beside his castle of Birmingham. The buildings would then have been of timber but the Birminghams are known to have had a stone-built fortified house on the site in the later medieval period. The family briefly lost the manor after one of them was killed fighting for the de Montforts at the Battle of Evesham in 1265. Another was ejected by Sir Edmund Ferrers in 1424 during an ownership dispute.

The last of the Birmingham family surrendered the manor to Henry VIII in 1536 in return for a pension, having got into debt and been convicted of a felony. The manor was granted to Thomas Marrow in 1557, and was sold by his descendants in 1746 to the Archers. Some of the medieval outbuildings seem to have still stood c1740 when the manufacturer John Francis built a new house within the moat. Hanson's plan of Birmingham of 1778 shows five separate structures standing in the western half of the site, and also shows the former parsonage site 200m south-west of St Martin's Church as being a platform about 30m across within a wet moat about 8m wide. All the buildings had gone by 1816 when the wide moat around a platform about 65m across was filled in and Smithfield Market built on the site. Excavations undertaken after the market was demolished in 1959 found footings of an ashlar faced wall of an apartment of some importance of the mid 13th or early 14th century.

Brailes *10 miles west of Banbury.*

On a small hill with extensive views except to the north is a motte now about 4m high and 25m across on top set in the middle of a pear-shaped platform 90m long by 60m wide which were built by the Earl of Warwick probably c1140.

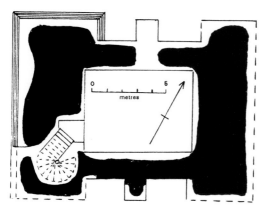

Plan of the keep at Brandon Castle

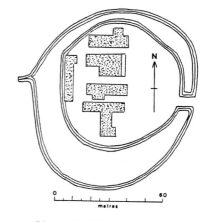

Plan of the Birmingham Moat

Brandon *Between Coventry and Rugby.*

The Clintons had a motte and bailey castle here in the mid 12th century. It passed to Nicholas de Verdon, generally credited as the builder of the keep on the motte, and who in 1226 raised the levels of the extensive system of moats fed from the adjacent River Avon. The castle does not appear to have been restored after being captured and destroyed in 1266 during a sortie by the rebel garrison of Kenilworth Castle. Neither of the moated enclosures now remaining in a private field seems to have had a stone wall. Only a defaced fragment of the keep now stands above ground level although excavations have revealed all of the basement of the unusually shaped building. It was a rectangle of 16.8m by 12.6m overall with end walls up to 4.5m thick. The side walls would be 3.3m thick but for being recessed either side of a central buttress possibly intended to carry arches further up. The entrance was presumably in the north wall at hall level. From there a spiral stair in the south-west corner led down to the dark storage basement and up to a possible third storey and the battlements.

Bretby *3 miles east of Burton upon Trent.*

Only extensive shapeless earthworks south-west of the church towards Bretby Farm remain of a castle which was dismantled by Philip Stanhope. His much altered new mansion of c1610 stands in extensive grounds nearby.

The site of Bridgnorth Castle from the railway station.

The Keep, Bridgnorth Castle

Site plan of Bridgnorth

Bridgnorth *Close to town centre.*

The sandstone promontory rising dramatically above the River Severn is a natural site for a fortress and may have been used for one of Ethelfleda's fortified towns of 910. In the 1070s Roger de Montgomery chose a more cramped and more vulnerable sandstone outcrop just downstream at Quatford for the site of a motte and bailey castle, collegiate church, and borough, supposedly in fulfilment of a vow made during a difficult crossing of the English Channel. However, his son Robert de Bellesme, noted as a military engineer, transferred all three to Bridgnorth in 1101-2 on the eve of his rebellion against Henry I. The latter eventually captured the castle and subsequently granted it to Hugh de Mortimer. Hugh was a noted supporter of King Stephen, and when Henry II succeeded Stephen in 1154 he insisted on the surrender of the Mortimer castles of Bridgnorth, Cleobury, and Wigmore as a token of good faith. This was refused and Bridgnorth was besieged and captured by the King in 1155. The ringwork and bailey known as Panpudding Hill on the other side of the Severn Valley Railway Station from the castle, is thought to have been a siegework used by the attackers as a base camp to protect them against sorties during this campaign.

33

The Pipe Rolls of Henry II record heavy expenditure on refortifying Bridgnorth Castle in 1166-74. The original form of the castle is unknown. The provision of a stone wall using blocks taken out of a rock cut ditch isolating the end of the promontory seems likely, although there is doubt as to whether de Bellesme would have had sufficient time to build elaborate masonry structures. Henry II provided such a wall or repaired an existing one and erected a square tower keep midway along its length to command the adjacent gateway. Although cracked and leaning as a result of being undermined and blown up in 1646, part of this keep still stands 16m high, almost the height of the wall-walk. The building measured 12.7m by 11.6m above a chamfered plinth from which rise pilaster buttresses. The vulnerable north wall is 2.9m thick and without openings. A stair in a forebuilding on the south side led up to the hall, above which was the King's private chamber, and below it was a dark basement. A spiral stair in the destroyed south-east corner connected all the storeys and also led to the battlements. Henry II also laid out the outer bailey on the site of the original town centre, the present High Street further north being presumably laid out c1170.

In 1211 King John added a barbican and turning bridge at the entrance to the outer bailey. During Henry III's minority from 1216 onwards the town was provided with a ditch and turf rampart, and in the 1260s this was partly augmented by a stone wall on the vulnerable north and west sides. To the east a mere breastwork would have sufficed. Additions and repairs were made to the domestic buildings of the castle during his reign, but in 1281 a report made for Edward I gives a long list of defects. The hall, chamber, King's kitchen and Queen's chamber were all dilapidated, timber had been stolen from a collapsed stableblock, and the drawbridge was said to be unable to carry the weight of a knight on horseback. Edward I was at Bridgnorth in 1294 and 1295, and Edward II came in 1321 so presumably some repairs were carried out.

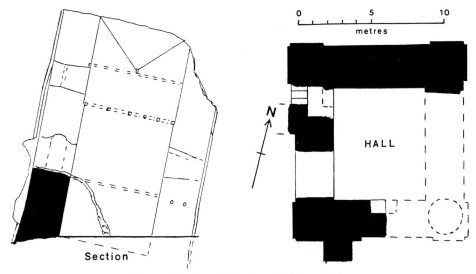

Plan and section of the keep, Bridgnorth Castle

During the 15th century Bridgnorth Castle was neglected and little used. By the time Leland saw it c1540 it was very ruined and the town had begun to encroach upon the outer bailey. King Charles came in 1642, admired the walks below the walls and installed a garrison, which finally surrendered in April 1646 after a long winter siege during which the walls were undermined. They were then dismantled and their materials plundered. The chapel of St Mary Magdalene by the public garden containing the keep was rebuilt as a parish church in 1792.

Brinklow   *6 miles east of Coventry*

This impressive motte with a pair of baileys measuring 180m by 100m overall across the substantial ramparts was probably built in the 1140s either by the Earl of Leicester or his tenants the Mowbrays. William de Stuteville obtained it after a lawsuit against the latter. It is not known if the site was still in use by the 1270s when it passed to the Wake family. There is public access to the site via a stile from an adjacent lane.

Bromwich   *5 miles north-east of Birmingham*

Overlooking the River Tame and junction 5 on the M6 north of the church is a mound which is all that remains of an earth and timber fortress held by the de Bromwichs as tenants of the Lords of Dudley. A high retaining wall has been built against the mound because of a feeder road for the motorway being cut through on this side, which was where the bailey lay.

The motte at Castle Bromwich

Caludon *2 miles east of Coventry.*

Edward I licensed John de Segrave to crenellate his manor house of Caludon, to the north-east of Coventry, in 1305. The moat, now dry, and obliterated on the east, around the platform 70m long by 48m wide may date from then. The fragment of masonry still standing is more likely to be associated with further works carried out by John de Mowbray and his wife Elizabeth, heiress of John, Lord Segrave, after Edward III granted a second licence for fortifications here in 1354. The fragment stands a little way in from the north side and has windows corresponding to two bays out of what must once have been an impressive upper storey hall at least 20m long, below which were either offices or cellars.

In 1385 several of the outbuildings were recorded as being in need of repair. Thomas Mowbray, created Duke of Norfolk in 1397, was residing at Caludon in 1398 when he appeared at Gosford Green for the duel which Richard II had ordered him to fight with the Duke of Hereford after each accused the other of treason. In the event the King stopped the fight before it began and banished both Dukes from the kingdom. After Richard, Duke of York's widow the Lady Anne Mowbray died in 1481 Caludon passed to William, Lord Berkeley. In the 1580s Henry, Lord Berkeley is said to have remodelled the castle and further additions were made for Elizabeth, Lady Berkeley in the early 17th century. The castle was sold in 1631 to Thomas Morgan and was left to decay, possibly because of damage sustained during the Civil War. The estate passed to the Prestons, and Cliffords, and was broken up in 1815. Eventually Coventry Corporation acquired most of the land for housing but the castle site was kept clear as public recreation ground and is accessible any time.

Caludon Castle

Castle Donington   *8 miles south-east of Derby.*

The village street winds its way round the west and south sides of a platform 17m high and 70m across with a very high counterscarp bank, except to the east where there was probably an outer bailey. The earthworks are much obscured by buildings, trees and fences, and are not accessible. King John took the castle from John de Lacy in 1214 and destroyed it soon afterwards, although a hall probably of c1180 with pilaster buttresses survived until at least the 17th century, being shown on an engraving of that period. Donington passed to the Earls of Kent and was sold by Elizabeth I to George, Earl of Huntingdon.

Caverswall   *5 miles south-east of Stoke-on-Trent.*

The drained wide and deep moat and the lower parts of the walls are relics of the castle which Sir William de Caverswall was licensed to crenellate in 1275. He was Sheriff of Staffordshire in the 1260s and lived until 1292. The walls now barely rise above the courtyard 45m square which has an octagonal tower at each corner and another pair flanking the gateway on the east side. The original apartments would have been on the west side where the moat is widest. In the 14th century the castle passed to the Montgomeries, and in the early 16th century it passed by marriage to the Giffards. They lived at Chillington Hall and the castle was leased to a tenant farmer named Browne and fell into decay.

The wealthy wool merchant Matthew Craddock purchased Caverswall in c1615 and built a fine new house, probably designed by John Smythson, on the north side of the court. The upper parts of the towers were rebuilt with the plain mullioned windows then in fashion. The towers and the three storey house were crowned with balustrades but the house was embattled in the 19th century. A Royalist force captured Caverswall from the Parliamentarian Craddocks in 1645.

Caverswall Castle

Chartley Castle

Chartley *6 miles north-east of Stafford.*

Chartley belonged to the Earls of Chester from the end of the 11th century until 1232, when on Ranulph de Blundeville's death it passed via his third daughter Agnes to William de Ferrers, Earl of Derby. The earthworks, comprising a motte with rectangular inner bailey, a square outer bailey beyond, and an outer bank beyond the deep ditch, lie on a hill beside the Stafford to Uttoxeter road. They may be as early as the 1090s, and at any rate must have existed by the 1150s. The Ferrers family appear to have been associated with the site either as tenants or as constables from an early date, but it was the Crown that had the castle repaired and garrisoned in 1191-2, and the stone walls and towers are generally thought to have been built by Earl Ranulph himself. Probably they were under construction in 1223 when he quarrelled with Henry III and was obliged to surrender his castles for a while.

Surviving are the outer walls of two towers on the south side, the basement of a round keep, the footings of the curtain walls and a twin D-shaped towered eastern gatehouse and the circular north-eastern tower. The keep and towers were built on a large scale with very thick walls pierced with cross-shaped arrowloops with downward sloping triangular feet. The keep measures 10.7m within walls 3.7m thick and had a projecting round stair turret facing the bailey, which is about 70m long by 50m wide. The two standing towers have diameters of 12.5m and 11.7m with walling up to 4.2m thick. The straight inner walls facing the bailey were much thinner and have fallen. The tower rooms lack fireplaces or latrines, so they do not appear to have provided domestic accommodation, nor are there any signs of domestic buildings.

38

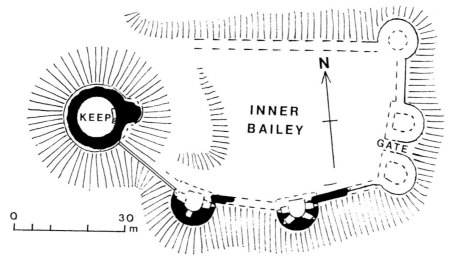

Plan of Chartley Castle

Robert de Ferrers, Earl of Derby, joined the de Montforts in their struggle against Henry III. After defeating Earl Robert in 1266 at Chesterfield the King gave Chartley to his younger son Edmund. Earl Robert seized the castle at night and held it until dispossessed by the King. Edward I finally returned the castle to Earl Robert in 1274. The family continued to hold Chartley until William, 6th Baron Ferrers, died in 1450, but it is doubtful if they ever resided in the castle which has no signs of any domestic buildings. Sir Walter Devereux, who was summoned to Edward IV's first Parliament in 1461 as Baron Ferrers of Chartley, having married the heiress Anne, and who was killed alongside Richard III at Bosworth in 1485, seems to have used an embattled timber mansion called Chartley Hall set within a moat about 90m square on the lower ground immediately west of the castle. Leland describes the castle c1540 as a ruin.

Sir Walter's great grandson the 1st Earl of Essex was a courtier of Elizabeth I. Mary, Queen of Scots, was confined at Chartley Hall from December 1585 until September 1586 when she was transferred to Fotheringhay Castle for trial and execution. One of the charges laid against Mary was she had plotted against Elizabeth, messages having been smuggled out of the hall to Anthony Babington in the false bottoms of beer casks. The 2nd Earl of Essex became Elizabeth's favourite in her old age but his rivals managed to get him posted to Ireland, accused him of treasonable dealings with the Queen's enemies there, and got him executed and attainted for rebellion in 1601. His son Robert was restored to the estates when James I came to the throne in 1603. Robert sided with Parliament in the Civil War but neither the ruined castle nor the hall are recorded as being involved in the conflict. In 1646 Chartley passed by marriage to the Shirleys, created Earls Ferrers in 1711, and owners until the 20th century. The hall was destroyed by fire in 1781 and the present house set on the west side of the moated platform dates only from 1847.

Cheswardine   *13 miles north of Telford*

The Le Strange family held Cheswardine from c1160. East of the church is a platform about 45m square within a wet moat 8m wide which is all that now remains of a castle thought to have been built by John le Strange c1310. A survey made upon his death in 1330 calls it a fortress of little strength.

Coventry   *By St Michael's Church in city centre.*

The Earls of Chester were granted half of the town of Coventry c1090 and had an important castle north-east of St Michael's Church by 1143 when Robert Marmion of Tamworth seized the adjacent priory and fortified it against the Earl. King Stephen ordered the castle to be surrendered in 1146, and he was wounded during one of several skirmishes in the district in 1147 when the Earl tried to take the castle back, only to be repulsed. Stephen then demolished the castle but it must have been rebuilt either in the 1150s or 1170s as it is referred to in several charters of the reigns of Henry II and John. The castle seems to have been partly of stone by then but nothing now remains of it. Earl Ranulph (see Chartley) abandoned it for the greater seclusion at Cheylesmore to the south.

Dawley   *1 mile south of Telford town centre.*

To the south of Holy Trinity Church is the site of a house which the cleric William de Morton was licensed to embattle in 1316. It seems to have later passed to the Earl of Arundel, probably his overlord, and in the Civil War was captured by the Royalists in 1643, and abandoned and burnt by them in the summer of 1645. There are no remains. Spoil heaps have engulfed a farm later built on the site.

Dudley   *In zoo, immediately north of town centre.*

William the Conqueror gave extensive estates centred on Dudley to William FitzAnsculph c1071. The Domesday survey of 1086 states that "the said William holds Dudley and there is his castle", so the earthworks evidently existed by then. Early in the 12th century Dudley passed to Fulke Paganel, probably by marriage. Ralph Paganel defied King Stephen, who in 1138 came and laid the district waste, although the castle does not appear to have been taken. It was, however, destroyed by Henry II in 1175 because Gervase Paganel had supported the King's sons in their recent rebellion. Gervase later paid 500 marks to regain his lands and the royal favour and the fragments of early masonry on either side of the gateway passage and in the service range are probably of c1180-5. In 1194 he was succeeded by his sister's son Ralph de Somery.

Dudley
Castle

An attempt by Roger de Somery to refortify the site c1261 was prevented by royal officials until a licence for such was granted in 1264. Parts of the bailey wall may be of that period, but the unusual keep on the mound and most of the gatehouse date from the time of John de Somery, who succeeded as a minor in 1291, was knighted in 1306, and died in 1321. He was a notorious local tyrant, William de Beresford and other neighbours complaining of him "that he has obtained such mastery in the county of Stafford that no man can obtain law or justice therein; that he has made himself more than a king there; that no one can dwell there unless he buys protection from him either by money or assisting him in building his castles, and that he attacks people in their own houses with the intention of killing them unless they make fine for his protection". Although half of it was destroyed to the base in 1647 his keep is an interesting instance of an early tower house, a self contained residence designed to impress and overawe the neighbouring lords. It is nearly 22m long by 15m wide and contained just a single main living room over a basement divided into storage and office space. The doorway was closed by a portcullis operated from two of the living room windows. Extra rooms providing sleeping and service spaces lay within four large round corner towers through the outer walls of which the main wall-walk was carried in galleries. The towers then rose a storey higher to provide fighting platforms above the galleries reached by ladders.

In 1321 Dudley passed to Margaret de Somery, wife of John Sutton. They got heavily in debt to John de Charlton, who, probably on the strength of a loan, was in possession of the castle in 1329 when it was besieged by number of neighbouring lords. Despite their financial difficulties the Suttons managed to build a new hall and apartment block on the east side of the bailey in the mid 14th century. Although gutted and somewhat altered the apartments remain fairly complete and include a chapel. The barbican with twin round turrets in front of the gateway, and probably also the thin enclosing wall of the outer court with a square gatehouse and one round corner tower, date from c1375-90.

41

Keep, Dudley Castle

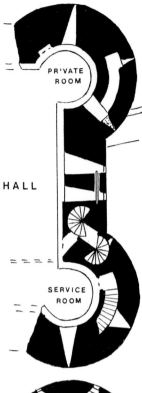

PRIVATE ROOM

HALL

SERVICE ROOM

BATTLE MENTS

0   6
metres

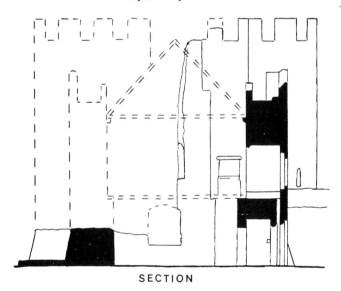

SECTION

Plans and Section of The Keep of Dudley Castle

42

The motte and keep at Dudley Castle

The sixth successive John de Sutton served Henry VI as a Lord Lieutenant of Ireland. He was wounded at the battle of St Albans and was incarcerated for a short while by Edward IV in the Tower of London. His grandson was the unpopular Edmund Dudley who did so much to build up Henry VII's fortune and was executed by Henry VIII in 1510. However, Edmund's son John rose high in the royal favour and was successively created Viscount Lisle, Earl of Warwick, and Duke of Northumberland. After he obtained the castle in the 1530s he remodelled the hall and built a splendid new set of apartments to the north of it. These are now roofless but otherwise intact and have mullion and transom windows, a polygonal stair turret facing the court, and incorporate a second gateway lacking the portcullis grooves featured in the main gateway arches.

Old Print of Dudley Castle

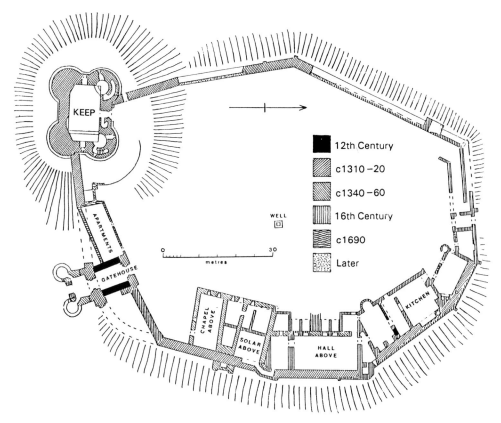

KEEP

12th Century

c1310-20

c1340-60

16th Century

c1690

Later

WELL

APARTMENTS

GATEHOUSE

CHAPEL ABOVE

SOLAR ABOVE

HALL ABOVE

KITCHEN

metres

Plan of Dudley Castle

John Dudley, Duke of Northumberland, was executed by Queen Mary in 1553 after his abortive attempt to have his daughter-in-law Lady Jane Grey crowned as the Protestant heir to Edward VI. In 1554 Dudley was granted to his kinsman Edward Dudley, who in 1575 entertained Queen Elizabeth at the castle. It was considered as a possible place of confinement for Mary, Queen of Scots, but was never used as such. The male line of the Sutton Dudleys failed in 1643 and the castle passed to the Wards. Thomas Leveson garrisoned it for King Charles in 1643 and in 1644 it withstood a siege by the Earl of Denbigh. In 1646 it was eventually surrendered without a siege to Sir William Brereton, and in 1647 the fortifications were dismantled. The apartments remained intact, however, and in the 1690s Edward Ward, Lord Dudley, built a new apartment block between the keep and gatehouse, thus partly obscuring the original access up to the keep and the low chemise wall which surrounded it. It was only when a fire gutted the apartments in 1750 that the Wards finally left Dudley for Himley. The castle ruins are open to the public as part of the zoo. Seals now inhabit the former moats.

Earl Shilton   *Between Nuneaton and Leicester.*

The 8m high mound in a field west of the church is assumed to have been raised in the 1140s by Robert, Earl of Leicester. The castle was presumably later rebuilt in stone as it was only finally destroyed in the early 17th century.

Eccleshall   *West of village, 7 miles north-west of Stafford.*

Eccleshall was an early seat of the Bishops of Coventry and Lichfield. In 1200 Bishop Muschamp was licensed by King John to fortify his manor house on flat ground by a stream the north of the church. The original enclosure is thought to have been semi-circular and the present rectangular court was laid out by Walter Langton, Bishop from 1297 to 1321. He was Treasurer of England under Edward I but was thrown into prison by Edward II, although later restored to office. Of his work there remain the three storey nine sided north-east tower, the footings of the 2m thick curtain wall around a court 75m by 54m, the dry east and south arms of the moat, and perhaps the stone bridge with four breakwater buttresses on the south side. There were presumably towers on the other corners and on either side of a gateway in the south wall plus a hall and chambers on the north.

In 1642 Bishop Wright garrisoned the castle for Charles I. He died within it in 1643 while under siege from a Parliamentary force which occupied the parish church as a strongpoint. A Royalist force arrived to relieve the castle and was on the point of taking away the Bishop's body and the treasure within the castle when a troop of Parliamentary horse arrived from Stafford. The Royalists fled in confusion leaving only ten men in the castle which was taken shortly afterwards with a night attack upon the gateway. The defences were dismantled by order of Parliament in 1646, but the apartments remained in use, and in the 1690s Bishop Lloyd built the present house, still a private residence, on the west side.

Eccleshall Castle

Elmley   *On north slope of Bredon Hill, 4 miles South-east of Pershore*

Robert D'Abitot built a castle within a corner of the ramparts of an Iron Age fort high up on the brow of Bredon Hill in c1090. High ramparts and deep ditches enclose a pear shaped area about 150m long by 100m wide, the northern third of which was closed off as a triangular inner ward. After Robert's nephew Roger was disinherited for slaying a royal servant Elmley passed via the latter's sister Emmeline to her husband Walter de Beauchamp. His son William probably strengthened the castle during the wars of the 1140s. There remain footings of a stone curtain wall 1.6m thick and a rectangular tower keep on the line of the wall between the baileys probably built c1180. Elmley remained the foremost castle in Worcestershire and the chief Beauchamp seat until the family inherited the earldom and castle of Warwick in 1267. Elmley Castle was then left to decay and when surveyed in 1316 was regarded as worth nothing. Minor repairs only temporarily halted the decay. Leland c1540 describes a ruin and says that he saw stone being taken from it to repair Pershore bridge. The site can be visited but there is no direct easy path up from the village.

Fillongley   *6 miles north-west of Coventry*

There are two castle sites at Fillongley, the 12th century ringwork of Castle Hills, and the later heart-shaped moated platform of Castle Yard which can be reached by a path across fields and has a few tumbled fragments of stone structures. These are perhaps of the time of the licence to crenellate granted by Edward I to John, 1st Lord Hastings in 1301. The castle was probably left to decay after the last of his line, another John, died in 1389, leaving Fillongley to the Bergavenny Beauchamps who had numerous other seats.

Fulbrook   *5 miles south-west of Warwick.*

A moated site west of Court Farm may be the site of a manor house held in 1324 by John de Hastings, Lord Bergavenny. It passed to John de Grey in 1389 and shortly afterwards was described as a hall with a solar and chapel adjoining with a kitchen and byre under one roof with on the other side of the moat a gatehouse and stable with a chamber above. The farmhouse west wall may be a relic of a new gatehouse built by Joan, Lady Bergavenny, in 1412. In the 1420s John, Duke of Bedford built a "praty castle made of stone and brike" in the field called Castle Hill to the south. It reverted to the Crown on the Duke's death in 1435, and again on the attainder of George, Duke of Clarence, in 1478, when it was described as ruinous. In the 1520s Sir William Compton was allowed to remove materials from the ruin to his house at Compton Wyniates. Nothing now remains although bricks, tiles and foundations have been found.

Gilmorton *10 miles south of Leicester.*

West of the church is a mound rising 6m to a summit 22m across. Beyond it to the west and south is a bean shaped bailey but the defences are mostly worn away except to the south-west. The castle was probably destroyed either under the terms of the treaty of 1148 between the Earls of Leicester and Chester or by Henry II after the 1173 rebellion. In the 13th century it was replaced by a manor house within a rectangular moated platform close by to the north-west.

Gresley *3 miles south of Burton upon Trent.*

All the stonework vanished long ago but a mound called Castle Knob remains of the seat of the Gresley family, owners since the time of Domesday Book.

Groby *5 niles north-east of Leicester.*

The 6m high oval mound east of the church was assumed to date back to the time of Hugh de Grentemesnil until excavation showed that it had been raised over a stone building so a date c1140 is more likely. It belonged to Robert de Ferrers at the time of the 1173 rebellion after which it was destroyed by Henry II. To the north are sections of double moats of a bailey of uncertain shape and size and beyond to the north-east is a later rectangular manorial moated site.

Hanley *West of the Severn 7 miles south of Worcester.*

Only a D-shaped platform 100m across with a deep ditch on the west and a shallower one on the south remains of a castle built at a cost of £750 by King John in 1207-12 as a hunting lodge. It was granted by Henry III c1220 to Gilbert de Clare and after the last of that line was killed in 1314 the castle went to the Despencers. It was damaged by the rebel barons in 1321-2. The heiress Eleanor de Clare was still living at the castle in the 1340s long after her husband's execution in 1326. In 1416 Richard le Despencer's widow Eleanor was granted the use of the following parts of the castle..."a great room at the end of the hall to the west with two towers of stone anex'd the said hall with one third of the pantry and buttery under the said room...two rooms called le guesten chambres, three towers in the south of the castle with a fourth tower in the corner of the castle towards the south,...a third of the bakehouse and kitchen adjacent to said tower...with a third of the palisade and moat around the castle". She had the use of the chapel and the third of the garden of the manor and a third of the park, but had to pay a third of the constable's fees. It is obvious from this that a large building with many chambers, outbuildings and towers once stood upon the site.

Hanley Castle later passed to the Earls of Warwick. In the 1480s repairs are recorded to the chapel, mill, kitchen, gatehouse, and drawbridge. In the early 16th century the castle was back in royal hands, firstly in the custody of Sir John Savage, and then under Sir William Compton, who was allowed to dismantle the buildings for their materials. Roland Badger owner the site later in the century. In the 17th century Habington wrote that the "castel is so vanished as theare appearethe nothinge in that place but a littel rubbyshe and a silly barne", but one tower stood until 1795 when it was demolished by the owner Thomas Hornyold to provide stone for repairing the bridge at Upton-upon-Severn. A house built upon the site was destroyed by fire in 1904 and has also vanished. A considerable section of the footings of the outer wall 2.7m thick was exposed on the site in c1880 and an oven was also found.

Hartlebury *4 miles south of Kidderminster.*

Hartlebury was a seat of the Bishops of Worcester from Saxon times. In the 1250s Bishop Walter de Cantilupe dug a moat around the manor house. Embattled walls around a court about 140m long by 85m wide with corner towers and a gateway on the east side were built by Bishop Giffard after a licence to crenellate was granted by Henry III in 1268, although the chief surviving relic of that period is the altered chapel. The gatehouse was rebuilt in the mid 15th century by Bishop Carpenter, and the walling of the hall and the saloon south of it is probably of the same period. Hartlebury is one of the few Midland castles described as in good repair by John Leland c1540, and was then the principal seat of the bishops.

Hartlebury Castle

48

In 1646 William Sandys installed a Royalist garrison of 120 foot and 20 horse with twelve months provisions in Hartlebury Castle, but in May it was surrendered to Colonel Thomas Morgan after just a two day siege. It was sold to Thomas Westrowe in 1647, and used as a prison for Royalist plotters in 1648. Shortly afterwards the defences were dismantled. Of them only two sides of the moat, one dry and the other still water filled, now remain. The castle was returned to the Bishop after the Restoration. The north-east wing, the central porch, the long gallery on the west, and many other fireplaces and windows are relics of remodelling in the 1670s by Bishop Fleetwood. In 1745 Bishop Maddox provided the chapel with a pretty fan vault and new windows at a cost of £1,200, and various other works were carried out in the 1750s, the 1760s, and the 1780s. In 1905-18 Bishop Yeatman Biggs created a college for clergy from a former stable block, and in 1964 the north wing and adjoining rooms were taken over by Worcester County Council for conversion into a County Museum.

Hartshill   *3 miles north-west of Nuneaton.*

On a ridge north of the village is a motte and bailey castle thought to have been built by Hugh de Hartshill c1140. The motte was abandoned long ago and is heavily overgrown. The bailey remained in use and in the early 14th century was provided by John de Hartshill with a wall, now ruinous, about 1.2m thick with crossloops at ground level at intervals of about 4.5m. A jamb of the gateway remains on the south-east, and in the middle of the north-east side, facing the motte, is a chapel with traces of a piscina. The castle subsequently passed to the Culpeppers, who sold it in the 1550s. One end wall with a projecting chimney breast survives of a house built within the north-east corner c1600. This was occupied by the Purefoys until they sold it to the Wrights in 1702. The bailey now forms a paddock serving a new house built outside the walls to the east.

Old print of Hartshill Castle

Hartshill Castle

Heighley   *9 miles north-west of Stoke-on-Trent.*

Henry III gave Henry de Audley a dozen hinds to stock his park here in 1223 and the castle is assumed to be of that period, although it is not specifically mentioned until 1276. It was similar to the equally spectacularly sited castle of the Earl of Chester at Beeston in being placed on a sandstone cliff with a rock cut ditch and an assumed twin towered gatehouse facing the more level approach. Only footings remain of the curtain wall and just a single fragment of one of the gateway towers. Above the cliff on the east side is a low fragment of arcaded walling which formed one side of a vaulted cellar above which was probably a late 13th century solar. The castle was neglected in the 14th century but was used as a prison in 1534 and was slighted by Parliamentary troops in the Civil War to prevent any attempt by the Royalists to occupy so strong a position. The site is private and heavily overgrown.

Hinkley   *In the town centre, 4 miles north-west of Nuneaton.*

The very damaged ringwork 60m across and up to 11m high in a garden east of the church may go back to the time of Hugh de Grentemesmil, Sheriff of Leicester under William I. The castle is mentioned in the treaty of 1148 between the Earls of Leicester and Chester and was destroyed by Henry II in the 1170s. It was rebuilt but the buildings had gone by the 17th century. The site was later landscaped and an ornamental pool made within the south-east part of the moat.

50

Holt Castle

Holt *By the River Severn 6 miles north of Worcester.*

A new manor house was probably built after William Beauchamp gave Holt to his younger son John in the mid 13th century. The 14th century tower now forming a porch is a relic of an embattled house built by a descendant who was created Lord Beauchamp of Kidderminster by Richard II in 1387. It was probably left incomplete on his execution by the Lords Appellants in 1388. The house may have been similar to that built at Broncroft in Shropshire by Sir Simon Burley, another of Richard II's unpopular favourites, where there was a central two storey block with a hall and private chamber end to end above a kitchen and offices or cellars, and square three storey corner towers. In 1472 Holt passed to the Guise family who probably built the existing much altered hall block behind the tower. It has a solar cross wing at the north end, and there was once a service wing at the south end. The castle was sold in 1557 to Sir John Bourn, who in turn sold it in 1578 to Thomas Fortescue. It later passed to the Bromleys, who sold the castle in the 1760s to Thomas, Lord Foley, later Earl of Dudley. The castle is private but can be viewed from the approach road to the church.

Inkberrow *East of the village, 10 miles east of Worcester.*

The moated site east of the village is probably a relic of a house built by Gilbert Marshall in 1235. This was on or near the site of a castle built c1180-1200 by either his father William, Earl of Pembroke, or his uncle John, and destroyed by Henry III's forces after the revolt of Richard Marshal in 1233. The house passed by marriage to the Monchelseys in 1241. After their forfeiture in 1265 it went to William de Valence and then to the Hastings family. It was ruined by 1392.

Kenilworth   *West of the town, between Warwick and Coventry.*

In 1120 Henry I gave Kenilworth to his Chamberlain Geoffrey de Clinton who built a dam across a shallow valley to provide an artificial lake on one side of a motte and bailey castle. Henry II garrisoned the castle against his rebellious sons in 1173 and found it so useful that he later obliged Henry de Clinton to exchange it for estates elsewhere. Royal expenditure on the castle is recorded in 1184 and the keep and inner bailey walls were probably then under construction. Despite having had new windows inserted in the 1570s and the north wall destroyed to the base in 1649, the keep is one of the finest structures of its type in Britain. Measuring about 24m by 18m over walls over 4m thick above a massive stepped base said to enclose the original motte, it is also one of the largest. A forebuilding protected the steps up to the doorway into the higher of the two storeys which was a hall. Private rooms, latrines, and a spiral stair were provided within four large square corner turrets, and there is a well set into the wall.

Richard I had the castle put into a defensible state in 1189 before going off crusading, but the keep was probably left unfinished until the wall gallery with cross loops above roof level was added in John's reign. John visited Kenilworth frequently and built much of the outer bailey wall. His are the Swan Tower at the north-west corner which is octagonal above a square base, and the circular Lunn's Tower at the north-east corner with pilaster buttresses pierced by cross-loops like those on the keep. He is also thought to have raised the dam to enlarge the lake. Kenilworth was one of four royal castles which under the terms of Magna Carta were required to be surrendered to the barons as a surety for the King observing the terms, but as John still had a garrison there in 1216 it was probably never actually handed over.

Henry III spent minor sums on repairs but little used the castle and eventually gave it to his sister Eleanor. She married Simon de Montfort who was created Earl of Leicester in 1239. They built the Water Tower, and probably also added the twin round fronted towers to the late 12th century gateway, plus the large enclosure called The Brays which defends the south end of the dam. The Provisions of Oxford of 1258 forbade foreigners to hold royal castles, so Earl Simon then lost Kenilworth until he seized power after defeating Henry III in battle at Lewes in 1264. Prince Edward was held within the castle as a hostage later that year. The Prince escaped from custody at another castle in 1265, mustered an army, and surprised and defeated an army under the Earl's son Simon encamped by the castle. The latter was obliged to swim across the moat in his night attire to escape capture. Soon afterwards the royal army defeated Earl Simon at Evesham. Simon the Younger left the castle later in the year and ordered the rebels within to surrender, but they feared their fate at the hands of the angry King and Prince and refused. Thus was set the scene for one of the most remarkable sieges ever mounted in Britain.

The castle was loosely blockaded during first half of 1266 and then closely invested by Henry and Edward until starvation and lack of munitions induced the rebels to surrender on honourable and favourable terms at Christmas time. The whole affair demonstrates just how effective a broad expanse of water could be in defending a large, strong, well stocked fortress held by a resolute garrison. Mining or scaling the walls was impossible. Wooden towers built to command the outer wall were shattered by stones from catapults within the castle. Barges were brought overland from Chester at great expense and trouble for an unsuccessful attack across the lake. When excommunicated by the Archbishop of Canterbury the garrison had one of their number dressed in a white shirt mock the archbishop by excommunicating him in turn. At the end the garrison were technically undefeated by force of arms and were allowed to march out into exile keeping their arms and armour instead of being hanged as they might otherwise have expected.

Kenilworth Castle

53

In 1267 Henry III gave Kenilworth to his younger son Edmund, Earl of Lancaster. During his tenure his castellan Roger Mortimer, after whom the gatehouse is named, organised at the castle a spectacular tournament with tilting on the dam. The foundations of a chapel with an east apse in the outer ward are relics of a college founded by Thomas, 2nd Earl, but left incomplete on his execution by Edward II in 1321. It was at Kenilworth in 1326 that the King was forced to abdicate in favour of his teenage son, and the castle was then restored to Thomas's brother Henry, whose son Henry was later created Duke of Lancaster. Edward III's third son John of Gaunt married the Duke's heiress Blanche and in turn became Duke of Lancaster. In the 1380s he built a splendid new hall 27.6m long by 14m wide which was one of the finest medieval secular apartments in Britain. It lay over a vaulted basement and was reached by a flight of steps up to a porch leading onto the screens passage at the north end. A small court separated the steps from a huge kitchen of the same period. The western corners of the hall block were built up as tower-like wings with octagonal corner turrets, that on the south containing a lobby giving access to a splendid series of apartments, now very ruined. These have an oriel turret towards the court and a latrine tower facing the field.

Old print of John of Gaunt's Hall at Kenilworth

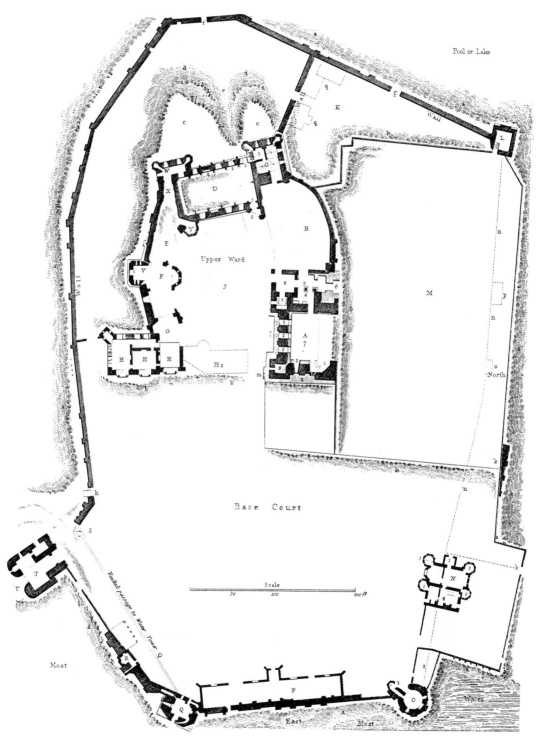

Old Plan of Kenilworth Castle

Mortimer's Tower, Kenilworth Castle

John of Gaunt's son became Henry IV when Richard II was deposed in 1399, and his grandson Henry V built a moated timber summer house with a harbour at the north end of the lake in 1414. This building, known as The Plesaunce, was dismantled and reconstructed within the outer ward for Henry VIII in the 1520s. A new range, now destroyed, was built on the east side of the inner ward at the same time. Kenilworth was later granted to John Dudley, newly created Duke of Northumberland. It reverted to the Crown after his execution by Queen Mary in 1553 but his son Robert gained favour with Elizabeth I and obtained Kenilworth and many other estates from her in 1563, and the earldom of Leicester in 1564. The Queen was entertained by the Earl three times at Kenilworth, the last occasion being in July 1575 when she stayed for eighteen days of hunting, dancing, allegorical presentations and other elaborate and expensive amusements. To provide extra accommodation for the Queen and her numerous attendants Robert Dudley added the tall four storey block since known as Leicester's Building at south-west corner of the inner ward. Also the keep was remodelled, large mullion and transom windows being inserted in place of the former narrow slits and some fresh chambers being created in the turrets. Earl Robert also built the long stable block on the east side of the outer ward, provided a new northward facing gatehouse with octagonal corner turrets, and laid out the recently reconstructed garden on the north side.

A survey made shortly after Kenilworth Castle reverted to the Crown early in James I's reign comments favourably on the quality and quantity of accommodation available within it, which was said to be adequate for simultaneous visits by the King, Queen, and Prince Henry with their households. In 1642 King Charles made no attempt to secure it, perhaps because the military value of the castle had been reduced by the Earl of Leicester's alterations on the north side, which may have included filling in parts of the moats protecting this vulnerable quarter. The castle was occupied by Parliamentary troops but did not see any fighting. It was slighted in 1649 just after a visit by Dugdale, who made some useful drawings of the castle published in 1658. The dam was breached to drain the lake to provide pasture, and Leicester's gatehouse was converted into a residence for Colonel Harksworth who purchased the estate for £2,000. It remained a private residence until recently. Sir Walter Scott's novel "Kenilworth" published in 1821 stimulated public interest in the ruins which passed into state guardianship (now English Heritage) just before World War II.

Kingsbury *By the church, 6 miles east of Sutton Coldfield.*

A promontory above a steep drop to the River Tame north of the church was fortified by the de Bracebridge family in the 14th century. To the east and south of a house of c1500 with additions made by the Willoughbys in the 1590s and later owners the Astons, are lengths of curtain wall 1.6m thick and 6m high. In the angle between them is a small polygonal tower with a latrine projection on the west side. The other end of the south curtain ends in another latrine projection, so there was perhaps once another tower there. In front of the rebuilt entrance arch now leading into a yard with various farm buildings there was once a tower or barbican and probably a drawbridge across the moat on this side.

Curtain wall and gateway at Kingsbury Hall

Kirby Muxloe   *In the village, 10 miles east of Leicester.*

William, Lord Hastings began building a splendid new castle of brick with stone dressings here in 1480. It was left incomplete after he was executed by Richard, Duke of Gloucester in June 1483. Most of it is reduced to footings standing little higher than the 17m wide wet moat, but the rectangular gatehouse with four octagonal corner turrets, the two innermost of which contain staircases, stands two storeys high, and the 7.5m square west tower of three storeys stands complete. Both structures contain gunports comprising round holes with sighting slits above, and required considerable repair after being taken into state guardianship in 1911. The gatehouse brickwork has decorative motifs including the initials of the builder and the sleeve which appears on his coat of arms. The west tower has square turrets where the curtain walls adjoined it, one containing a stair and the other small rooms and latrines, and both rising one stage higher. This layout was repeated in the other three corner towers. There were four ranges of apartments around a central court, the hall and kitchen being in the south-east range opposite the gatehouse. The central projections which occur in the low outer walls overlooking the moats may not have been repeated in the outer walls of the apartments, although there could have central bays or towers. During site clearance footings of an earlier hall were found in the middl;e of the court. It dated from about the time when the Hastings family acquired Kirby in the mid 14th century. A fairly complete set of buildings accounts survive and from them we know that the earlier house had a moated court with a gatehouse and corner towers as at present, although laid out on more modest lines. The present corner towers were rapidly erected during 1482 but the gatehouse, which was intended to have a machicolated parapet, was still unfinished in September 1484 when it was given a temporary covering of thatch.

Kirby Muxloe Castle

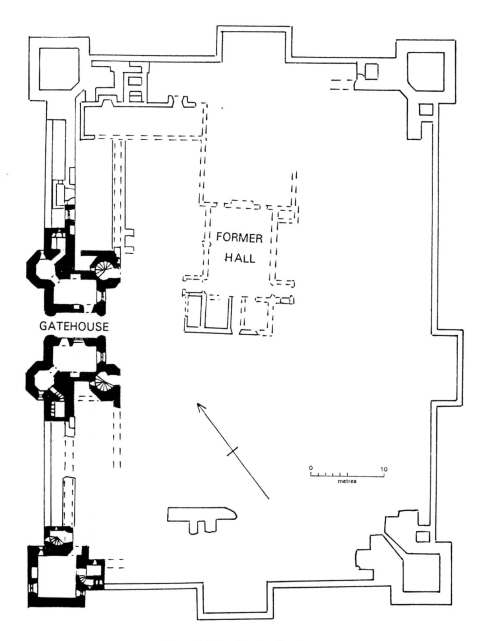

FORMER HALL

GATEHOUSE

metres

Plan of Kirby Muxloe Castle

Langley   *2 miles east of Sutton Coldfield.*

Only traces of the former moats now remain of the house which Edward III permitted Edmund de Beresford to fortify in 1327. It subsequently passed to the Hores, Pudseys, Jessons, Pearsons, and Lynches. Footings of stone walls and later brick walls were visible early in the 20th century when one side of the moat was filled in. A stable block of much later date is converted to apartments.

Leicester   *By the river on the west side of the city centre.*

Leicester Castle was founded by William I probably in 1068, and was put in the custody of Hugh de Grentemesnel. His son Ivo was fined so heavily for rebellion against William II that his estates had to be mortgaged to Robert de Beaumont who eventually took possession. De Beaumont is thought to have been made Earl of Leicester by Henry I and may have begun to refortify the castle in stone. The still surviving church of St Mary de Castro, which was originally the castle chapel lying in the middle of the bailey, retains parts of a large cruciform building of c1120. A fine aisled hall with stone walls and timber arcades built c1150 still stands on the west side of the bailey overlooking the River Soar, having survived the destruction of the castle defences in 1173 after the then Earl joined the rebellion of Henry II's sons and the castle was captured after a siege lasting several weeks. It is in a much altered state after having long remained in use as an assize court. The east wall was rebuilt in brick in 1690 and in 1821 the interior was divided into two courtrooms with ancillary chambers, further alterations being made in 1856.

The castle and earldom passed to the de Montforts in the early 13th century and after their fall in 1265 (see page 49) were granted by Henry III to his own younger son Edmund. His son Thomas repaired the castle and frequently resided there. Edward I came to stay in 1300, and Edward II in 1310 and 1311. The castle was also a favoured residence of Edward III's son John of Gaunt who built the cellar surviving south of the hall. There was probably a kitchen above, and the private chambers lay on the north side of the court. Richard II visited the castle in 1390 and it became royal again on Henry IV's accession after which the inner bailey walls were rebuilt. From that era remain the precinct walls to the south of St Mary de Castro which isolated the church from the main court, a timber framed gateway north of the church, and a modest ruined gatehouse which gave access to an outer enclosure on the south called the Newark which contained a college founded by Earl Henry in 1330. Two buildings which lay within that court survive in a much altered state and there is also the so-called Magazine Gate, probably 15th century, which led out of the Newark towards the town, and which now lies isolated within a complex of modern roads. The motte also survives to a height of 9m but until 1840 was somewhat higher. Visitors can reach the mound summit by means of a path from the gardens to the west.

Bailey Gateway, Leicester Castle   The Newark Gate, Leicester

Lichfield   *In town centre.*

The castle built in 1129 and destroyed under the terms of a treaty of 1148 probably stood in the area of Ware Street and Frog Street. The cathedral close is protected by a formidable ditch 30m wide by 5m deep on the east and north and there is pool to the south. The ditch cut by Bishop Roger de Clinton in the 1130s was probably widened after Edward I in 1299 licensed Bishop Walter Langton to provide the close with an embattled wall. The remains comprise the north and east curtain wall footings, one wall of the west gate tower, an altered tower in the south-east corner with a polygonal turret on the outer angle, and the recently excavated base of one of the polygonal towers flanking the south gate. The close was garrisoned for King Charles in 1642. In March 1643 Lord Brooke was fatally wounded whilst leading an attack on the south gate. Sir John Gell continued the attack with a bombardment from the south and the garrison submitted two days later. Prince Rupert recaptured the close after a ten day siege shortly afterwards and King Charles visited it three times during 1645. Sir William Bereton besieged the close from April 1646 until mid July when the garrison of 700 men with 85 officers and a number of refugees surrendered on terms allowing them to leave with their arms. During the siege cannon fire destroyed the central spire of the cathedral and by 1649 the close wall, the cathedral, and the Bishop's Palace in the north-east corner had all been wrecked.

Mackworth   *At west end of village, 3 miles north-west of Derby.*

The thin front wall with a four centered arch of an embattled gatehouse of 1495 is all that remains of the seat of the Mackworths' probably destroyed in the Civil War. In 1655 the site was sold by Sir Thomas Mackworth to Sir John Curzon.

Madeley   *North of village, 7 miles west of Stoke-on Trent.*

In the north-east corner of a low lying platform with a wet moat partly surviving is a fragment of walling 1.7m thick with a gateway jamb containing a portcullis groove. Ralph, Lord Stafford was licensed to crenellate a manor house here in in 1348. It is uncertain whether it was a courtyard house or a tower.

Maxstoke   *8 miles north-west of Coventry.*

Maxstoke is one of the most complete of the smaller late medieval baronial castles of England. Slighting was considered in 1648 after the castle had held a Parliamentary garrison since 1643 but was not carried out. So the 2m thick curtain walls around a court 51m by 46m with a wet moat, four octagonal corner towers 9m in diameter, and the gatehouse on the east side with octagonal turrets facing the field and a rib-vaulted passage, all survive intact and little altered. The towers contain three storeys of rooms for retainers with latrines, fireplaces, and ogee headed windows. An exception is the north-west corner which is of four storeys and contained bedrooms above a vaulted strongroom. Originally the solar adjoined this tower with a chapel to the south. Beyond the chapel, for which a large west window was later pierced through the curtain wall, was the hall and south of that the service rooms, and a postern. In a late 15th century remodelling of the apartments a new hall was created in place of the original solar. Then or soon after, the ranges along the north and south sides of the court were dismantled leaving only scars on the outer walls. The apartments have seen various later alterations and the chapel is now subdivided.

Old print of Maxstoke Castle

The castle was built in the 1340s by William de Clinton, Earl of Huntingdon as a residence for his nephew and heir John. Dugdale claimed that a licence to crenellate was obtained from Edward III in 1346. A century later Maxstoke was obtained by Humphrey, 6th Earl of Stafford, later Duke of Buckingham, by an exchange of manors with John, Lord Clinton and Say. The Duke was killed in battle at Northampton in 1459, the 2nd Duke was executed by Richard III in 1483, and the 3rd Duke, restored to the honours by Henry VII in 1485, was executed by Henry VIII in 1521. The castle was then granted to Sir William Compton. In 1597 William, 2nd Lord Compton, conveyed Maxstoke to Sir Thomas Egerton. From him it passed to the Dilkes who lived in it until the 20th century. In 1745 part of the Duke of Cumberland's army was billeted in barns and outbuildings of the castle when he was on his way northwards to engage the Jacobite army led by Bonny Prince Charlie. The castle is still occupied as a private residence and neither it nor the grounds are open to the public.

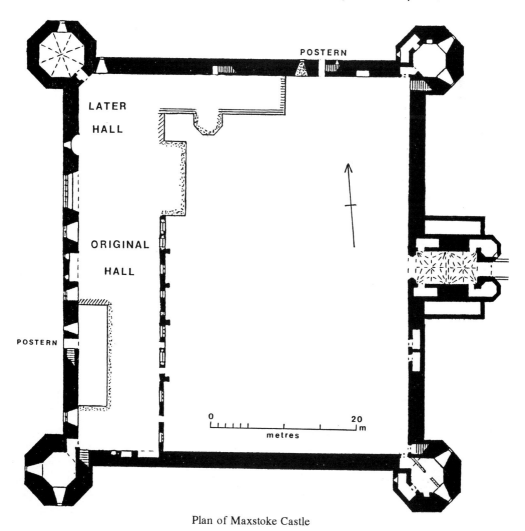

Plan of Maxstoke Castle

Melbourne   *7 miles south-south-east of Derby.*

Within a private garden remain a fragment of walling about 20m long by 5m high and the footings of a semi-circular turret of a castle built in 1311 by Robert de Holland. It is said to have had a square gatehouse and several other towers and unusual shaped chimneys above the ranges of apartments. The castle passed by marriage to John of Gaunt and remained part of the Duchy of Lancaster until it was given to the Earl of Nottingham in 1604. It later passed to the Earl of Huntingdon and the Marquis of Hastings. Within the castle the Duke of Bourbon, who was taken prisoner at the battle of Agincourt in 1415, was held captive for nineteen years until a huge ransom was paid.

Newcastle-under-Lyme   *West of town centre.*

Excavations revealed sections of walling but all that now remains visible of this once important castle is the much reduced mound between a factory and a bowling green beside Silverdale Road. Housing now occupies the site of the bailey to the north. The other sides were protected by a lake made by damming the Lyme Brook. Newcastle was founded either by Henry I or Ralph Gernons, Earl of Chester. The latter surrendered the castle after being captured by King Stephen in 1146 but it was returned in 1149. Ralph was murdered by William Peverel in 1154 and Henry II then took over the castle. The Pipe Rolls record it being garrisoned by the Crown and gradually rebuilt in stone until 1215 when it was granted to Ranulph, Earl of Chester. A 17th century account says the keep was twenty paces square and seventy feet high with three storeys, and that the outer curtain walls were heavily buttressed. Henry III gave Newcastle to his younger son Edmund, Earl of Lancaster. The castle was repaired by John of Gaunt and Henry IV but was neglected by Henry VI in favour of Tutbury. It was very ruined except for the keep when visited by John Leland in c1541.

Norbury   *9 miles west of Stafford.*

An irregularly shaped quadrangular platform with the footings of one metre thick ashlar faced retaining walls and a surrounding moat fed by a stream, now nearly dry, marks the site of a mansion built by Ralph Butler, lord of Norbury from c1291 to 1307. A drawing of the east front as it appeared in the 1680s survives showing a bridge leading to a central entrance. On either side were ranges with small lower windows, and there was a round bartizan corbelled out from the south-east corner. The mullion and transom windows of the two upper storeys south of the gate, and the jettied timber framed single upper storey of the range north of the gate must have been alterations carried out by the Skrymshers, owners from 1521 to 1775. The decayed house was demolished in 1838.

Old Sketch of Norbury Manor

Oversley   *Near Alcester, 7 miles south-west of Redditch.*

The Botelers or Butlers had their chief seat at Oversley as tenants of the Earls of Leicester until they transferred to Tyrley in Shropshire in the mid 13th century. Excavations suggested that the original timber buildings, later replaced in stone, were erected on virgin soil without any earthworks being constructed beforehand on the hilltop. There are no visible remains of the castle. A new house was built on the site in the late 16th century by the Parkers, tenants of the Cooks.

Ragley   *2 miles south-west of Alcester.*

In 1381 John Rous was pardoned for crenellating the gatehouse of his new house or castle at Ragley without licence and allowed to continue with the work. In 1523 Ragley passed by marriage to the Bromes of Halton, who sold the manor in 1591 to Sir John Conway. The 2nd Earl of Conway had the site cleared in the 1680s prior to the construction of the present Ragley Hall, which was remodelled by the Earls of Hertford in the mid and late 18th century.

Rodbaston   *Near Penkridge, between Stafford and Wolverhampton.*

The hereditary forester of Cannock had a castle in this area in 1154. In 1199 it is mentioned as a manor house, but another record of it in 1215 again calls it a castle. Not far from the Wolverhampton to Stafford road is a 6m wide water filled moat around a heavily overgrown platform 50m square with a mound of debris covering the footings of buildings on the south-east side. These works appear to date from the 1330s when John Saundersted built an embattled house at Rodbaston. From the 1380s until c1768 the house was occupied by the Egintons as tenants under a number of different families as overlords.

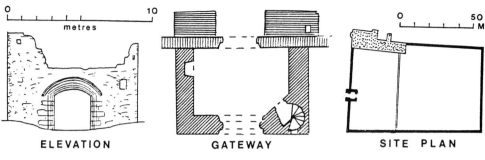

ELEVATION   GATEWAY   SITE PLAN

Plans of Rushall Hall

Rushall *2 miles north-east of Walsall.*

The hall has a court 90m long by 56m wide enclosed by a curtain wall up to
6.3m high in places but only 0.7m thick. This wall may have stood in 1323 when
Robert de Eslinton took refuge here with William de Boweles from a notorious
local trouble maker, John de Wetales, who was subsequently fined for shooting
arrows over the gate. Indeed the men working for de Boweles whose tools were
confiscated by officials of Cannock Forest may have been illegally quarrying
limestone for the walls. However the walls are perhaps more likely to be of
c1400 when "Geffrey Ive pulled down an old halle at Rushale, and set up a newe
hall" on the occasion of his daughter becoming the second wife of William
Grobbere. John Harpur married the heiress Eleanor Grobbere and he or his son
added the gatehouse against the entrance arch on the west gate of the court.
This gatehouse originally had just a single chamber reached by a spiral stair from
the passage below, but it was extended and provided with a latrine and a now
destroyed upper storey by the Leighs in the late 16th century.

Edward Leigh supported Parliament in the Civil War, and in 1643 Rushall Hall
was besieged and captured in his absence by the Royalists under Prince Rupert
despite a valiant defence by Lady Leigh and her servants. In May 1644 the hall
was besieged and captured by the Earl of Denbigh. He described it as "watered
round about, admirable works where are four forts at each end of the house one,
from the water to the top of the works is some four or five yards high, besides
the breadth of the trench, which answerable to it, and a stone wall within the
works much higher, besides a very strong drawbridge, and but only one passage
through the stone wall into the house, which is as strong as art can make, and
within the wall, in the yard, they have made galleries for their better defence,
and greate stones laid thick round the works, which upon any assault would
have done as much execution as the muskets." Scarcely any trace survives of
these earthworks. The hall passed to the Mellishes in 1811 and was eventually
let to a farmer who partly demolished the wall and gateway in order to burn the
stone to make lime. From 1857-89, however, the hall had a more sympathetic
occupant, the antiquarian W.H.Duignan. The house in the court is still a private
residence and neither it or the walls are open to the public.

Seckington   *North of church, 4 miles north-east of Tamworth.*

North of the church is a fine motte and bailey castle probably built in the 1130s or 40s by the Earl of Leicester. In c1170 Richard Bruton held it from the Earl and sold it to William de Campville. The motte has a summit 15m in diameter and rises 9m above a crescentic bailey 30m across with an entrance gap in the rampart and ditch towards the south-east.

Interior of north wall, Stafford Castle

Stafford   *1 mile west of the town centre.*

The motte and bailey castle which stood on the west side of the town within the area defended by the River Sowe is thought to have been that erected by King William in 1070. In the following year he granted many manors in Staffordshire to Roger de Toeni whose son adopted the surname de Stafford and built the existing castle on a hill some way to the west. Domesday Book suggests that the older castle was then destroyed and it is assumed that the fortress entrusted by Henry I to William Pantulf in 1102 was the new baronial castle. This site is mentioned in the 1140s and Robert de Stafford, who died in 1188, is thought to have added a stone tower keep on the mound. Hervey Bagot, who married Robert's heiress Millisent, adopted the Stafford surname to continue the line.

In 1347 Ralph, Lord Stafford made an agreement with the mason John de Burcestre for the construction of a substantial tower house on the mound. The shape of the latter was considerably altered to bear this structure which was 14.8m wide by 34.4m long over walls 2.7m thick and seems to have incorporated, or was built over the site of, the earlier keep. A licence to crenellate the building was granted in 1348. Apart from a wine cellar below the east end the building had just two storeys, one for the storage and preparation of food and drink and the use of servants, and the other forming a splendid and secure private suite for the lord. Four octagonal corner towers 9m in diameter appear to have contained four storeys of private rooms corresponding to the mostly solid basement filled by the stump of the original mound summit, each of the two main storeys, and the level of the wallwalk on the main block. A fifth tower in the middle of the south wall is known only from an old plan. We know from the contract of 1347 that the parapet was intended to be machicolated. The present westward facing entrance is said to lie on the site of a postern although it is not shown on an old plan. The main entrance was in the north wall but it is not clear how access up to the hall was obtained. There was a narrow service stair adjoining the north-west tower.

Inside of SW tower, Stafford Castle

South front, Stafford Castle

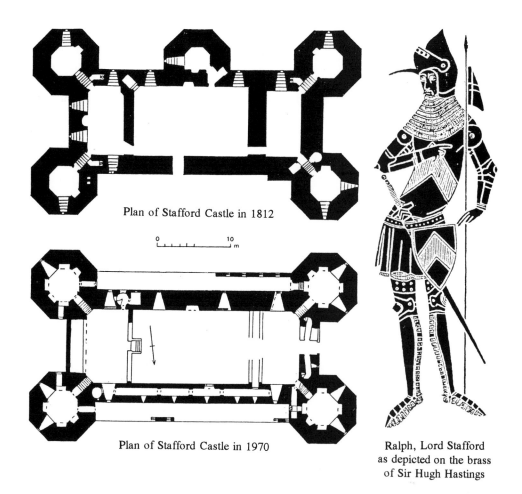

Plan of Stafford Castle in 1812

0   10
m

Plan of Stafford Castle in 1970

Ralph, Lord Stafford
as depicted on the brass
of Sir Hugh Hastings

When Edmund, Earl of Stafford was killed at the Battle of Shrewsbury in 1403 he left an infant heir Humphrey who eventually married into the Buckingham family, thus obtaining wide estates with many more castles and the Duchy of Buckingham. After Henry VIII executed the third Duke in 1521 on trumped up charges of treason, for no better reason than a plausible claim to the throne, the Stafford estates were surveyed. From this and another survey of 1537 we know some lost details of the buildings and their furnishings. In the bailey there were throughout the medieval period a suite of apartments, a kitchen, a stable block, a chapel of St Nicholas, barns, and other service buildings probably constructed from an assortment of materials. No evidence has ever been found that the bailey was fortified with a stone curtain wall. Despite the importance of the castle and continued use of the bailey buildings until the 16th century it seems that there was only ever a ditch and palisade. Elizabeth I was entertained to dinner at the castle in 1575 but it was subsequently neglected, being described as "rotten" in 1603, and "somewhat ruined" in 1634. The barony was surrendered by an impoverished heir to Charles I in 1639 and granted to Sir William Howard, husband of Mary Stafford.

Old print of Stafford Castle

When the Civil War broke out in 1642 the elderly Isabel, Lady Stafford was still living in the tower house. She fortified the castle for the king and recent excavations found evidence that the bailey, which is over 100m across, was regarded as too large an area to defend with the available forces. Part of it was refortified with earth and timber with the aid of gabions (wicker baskets filled with earth). After a minor skirmish nearby in May 1643 the castle was besieged by Parliamentary forces until July when the garrison withdrew. At the end of the year the castle was ordered to be "forthwith demolished".

In the 18th century the north-east corner tower, which remained standing higher than the rest of the tower house after destruction, was converted into a folly. A new Earldom of Stafford created for Henry Howard in 1688 became extinct in 1762 but in c1812-15 Sir George Jerningham, descended from the last Earl through the female line, began to rebuild the tower house on the understanding it would aid his claim to a peerage. By 1817 Edward Jerningham was inhabiting a suite of chambers at the east end and the towers at that end had been restored to about their original height. The remainder had been rebuilt to a lower level by 1824 when Sir George finally became Baron Stafford. It was then left open as a garden instead of being completed, as by then the family had realised the castle was never going to be as comfortable as any of their other residences.

The castle was gradually left to deteriorate again until it was declared unsafe in 1950 and the last caretakers left. In 1961 a boy playing at the castle was killed when the mullions of the main east window fell on him and Stafford Borough Council then demolished most of the upper parts. They resisted demands for total demolition and from 1978 began archaeological exploration and repair of the ruins and earthworks. Only then was it discovered for certain that the footings of the medieval tower house survived below the early 19th century superstructure. The ruins and earthworks are now open to the public.

Old Print of Stourton Castle

71

Stourton Castle

Old Print of Stourton Castle

Stourton   *Near Kinver, between Wolverhampton and Kidderminster.*

There was probably a hunting lodge in the royal forest of Kinver by the late 11th century. The lodge was provided with a ditch in 1184 and a palisade in 1185, and work was done on the buildings in 1187 and 1190. In 1195 it was transferred to the present site at Stourton. Timber buildings then erected included a hall and offices, a kitchen, a chamber, a gaol, a gate with a brattice, and a palisade 16 feet high with a circumference of 16 perches. King John came here to hunt in 1207 and 1215. By 1222 the lodge was known as the castle of Kinver and Henry III had the defences rebuilt in stone. Footings of two round towers on the circuit of the outer bailey wall were discovered in 1832. In 1316 Sir John Vaux, Keeper of Kinver Forest and Stourton Castle, was acquitted of the murder of his wife's previous husband Sir Thomas Murdak at the castle, although his wife Gillian was found guilty and sentenced to be burnt.

The oldest building now standing on the site of the small inner court upon an outcrop above the River Stour is a modest square tower similar to that at Holt. It was probably part of a stronghouse built either by Richard de Hampton in the 1380s or his son John in the 1390s. The latter was licensed to have an oratory at the castle in 1391. His son, another John, held a number of important offices under Henry VI and is thought to have rebuilt the castle. He lost his estates and offices when Edward IV seized the throne in 1461, but briefly recovered them in 1470 when Henry VI was restored for a short while.

The celebrated cleric Reginald Pole is thought to have been born at Stourton Castle c1500. His mother was a daughter of the Duke of Clarence, who was granted the castle by Edward IV in the mid 1470s, only to be executed in 1478 for treason. Reginald fell out with Henry VIII over the latter's divorce and went off to Rome where he was made a cardinal and sent to persuade Spain and France to invade England. He survived assassination attempts and returned to serve as Archbishop of Canterbury during Queen Mary's reign from 1553 to 1558. The brick ranges of the present structure at Stourton date from that period or a little later, although the gables are 17th century. There are very considerable alterations and extensions of various periods, particularly the 1830s when the porch tower of the hall was demolished.

During the first two thirds of the 17th century the castle was occupied by the Whorwood family who had another residence nearby at Compton until 1650. John Whorwood seems to have remained neutral in the Civil War but in 1644 Stourton Castle was captured by the Parliamentarian Colonel Thomas Fox. He was later routed on Stourbridge Heath by Sir Gilbert Gerard, Governor of Worcester, and the castle then fell to the Royalists. The defences were probably destroyed by order of Parliament in the late 1640s and 18th century views show a many gabled house standing on a platform with a buttressed retaining wall on the north and east, presumably the truncated original inner bailey curtain wall. Subsequently the castle was regarded as unfit as a residence for gentry because of noise and vibration from the adjacent mill so it was let as a farm to the Hollins family. In the 19th century it was occupied by a succession of industrialists. The castle was sold in 1974 and remains occupied as a private residence.

Strensham *Near motorway services 10 miles south of Worcester.*

The platform measuring 35m by 30m defended by concentric rectangular moats up to 12m wide probably dates from the time of Sir John Russell, Master of Horse to Richard II, who was licensed to crenellate his house here in 1388. The bank with angular corner bastions between the two moats presumably dates from the Civil War when Sir William Russell, created a baronet by Charles I in 1627, was the Royalist Governor of Worcester. The house was probably destroyed during the conflict and no walling now remains. The new seat of Strensham Court nearby was built in the 1660s and rebuilt in 1824.

Studley *By Studley parish church, 3 miles south east of Redditch.*

Throughout the medieval period the manor of Studley was held by a family called de Studley. Immediately north of the church is an early 16th century house built by Thomas Atwood within the circular moated enclosure of their castle or moated manor house. Part of the dry moat remains by the lane to the church.

Tamworth   *By town centre.*

On the strength of Tamworth having been the capital of Mercia from c760 to 943 the castle mound has sometimes been erroneously described as being of Saxon origin. However it is obviously a typical Norman defensive work no doubt raised in the 11th century by Robert Marmion. He held the office of Royal Champion which required the holder to attend coronations in full battle dress and "oppose himself against any person who should gainsay the royal coronation". The castle was rebuilt in stone in the 12th century and was ordered by King John to be destroyed in 1215 because Robert Marmion, 5th baron, sided with the barons against him, but this does not appear to have been carried out. The Marmion male line failed in 1294, and Edward I later granted the castle to Sir Alexander de Freville. He served as Royal Champion at the coronation of Edward III, technically a minor, in 1327. This is the only occasion when the office was actually recorded as being performed.

The mound stands at the north-west corner of a quadrangular bailey 90m long with east and west sides of about 35m and 60m respectively set on the north bank of the Tame. Excavations have revealed post holes of the original palisade around the bailey and footings of 16th century stables and outbuildings have been located near the bandstand. In 1972-4 the lowest stage of a heart shaped gatehouse of c1260 with a later bridge abutment on the north side of the bailey were revealed and left exposed. The surviving part was at moat level, the actual gateway being above, with at least one more storey on top. The upper portions were demolished c1700 and the lower part incorporated in the cellars of a public house removed c1970. Crossing the motte ditch on the east side is a section of curtain walling 2.7m thick upon which was the only access up to the keep. This wall has sections of herringbone masonry unlikely to be later than c1130.

The keep from the east, Tamworth Castle

Keep and motte from the south, Tamworth Castle

The polygonal shell wall of coursed rubble 2.3m thick above a high battered plinth which encloses a court 31m by 28m on the mound is likely to be of the same period as the approach wall, i.e. c1125-40. The mural stair on the south side probably led up to the original wall walk about 4m above the court. The shell was later heightened to a new wall-walk 7.4m above ground, protected by a parapet 3.8m high. Commanding the eastern approach and straddling the wall is a contemporary tower with walling 2m thick around an unlit basement about 4m square. The tower walls are thinner at the higher levels. The outer corners have typical Norman pilaster buttresses slightly set back which are finished off at the top by later medieval round turrets. The gateway adjoining the tower is a later insertion and is surmounted by a Jacobean building called the Warder's Lodge, now containing the ticket office. A window embrasure on the north side of the shell wall, facing the field, may be a the site of a former postern.

Originally there would have been lean-to buildings around the shell with the hall perhaps where the kitchen and service rooms now are on the north side. Walling in this part is perhaps older than the late 15th century hall running from north to south, parallel with, but clear of, the west side. This leaves a modest court between it and the gateway. The hall has been much remodelled and the entrance porch, the staircases at the south-west and north-east corners, and much of the domestic apartments to the south, are the work of Sir John Ferrers during James I's reign. Further alterations were carried out after the Civil War, and in the 18th century, notably the big northern bay windows.

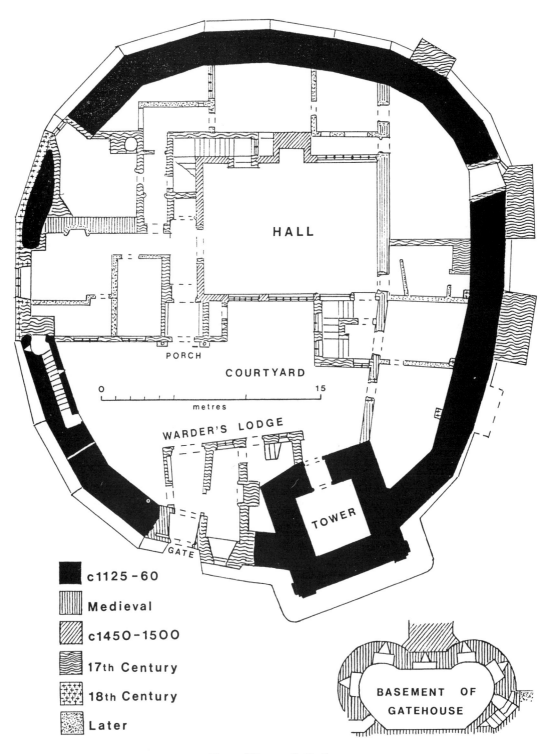

HALL

PORCH

COURTYARD

0   15

metres

WARDER'S LODGE

TOWER

GATE

c1125-60

Medieval

c1450-1500

17th Century

18th Century

Later

BASEMENT OF GATEHOUSE

Plans of Tamworth Castle

Hall Porch, Tamworth Castle   Herringbone Masonry, Tamworth Castle

In 1423 Tamworth Castle passed by marriage to Sir Thomas Ferrers, son of the 5th Baron Ferrers of Groby in Leicestershire. His successors continued to use the keep as an occasional residence, and were carrying out repairs to it on the occasion of John Leland's visit in 1541. He records that the "base-court and great ward of the Castle is cleane decayed and the wall fallen down, and theirin be now but houses of office of noe notable building". The castle was visited three times by James I and was garrisoned for Charles I in 1642. It was captured by Parliamentary forces in 1643 and somehow managed to avoid being slighted. In 1688 Ann Ferrers, heiress of Tamworth Castle, married Robert Shirley, heir of Baron Ferrers of Chartley, thus reuniting the two branches of the family. Their daughter and heiress married James Crompton, fifth Earl of Northampton, in 1715 and in 1751 another heiress brought the castle to George Townsend. These families had residences elsewhere and rarely used the castle. In the 1790s the hall in the keep was leased to the industrialist Robert Peel for use as a forge connected with his nearby factory. In 1897 Tamworth Corporation purchased the castle from Marquis Townsend, laid out the bailey as a public garden with a bandstand and renovated the keep, opening it in 1899 as the town museum.

Tong *By M54 9 miles north-west of Wolverhampton.*

This castle was probably founded by Richard de Belmeis, Bishop of London, who was granted the manor of Tong by Henry I in the 1120s. It consisted of a ringwork 30m wide by 40m long set on a low promontory between two streams. The original access to the castle is thought to have been from the west across the streams but a new approach from the east was created by the La Zouch family who built a stone wall around the court probably in the 1170s or 80s. Early in the 13th century the La Zouches added a spacious new outer bailey. Excavations revealed part of the outer bailey east wall with the base of round south-east corner tower 7m in diameter and what was assumed to be a central rectangular gatehouse, but these may have dated from the time of a licence to crenellate issued by Richard II in 1381.

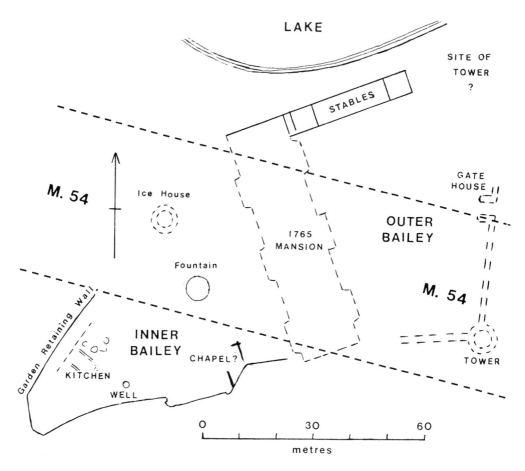

Plan of Tong Castle

78

What happened to these early fortifications is a puzzle. Perhaps they were destroyed during Henry III's struggles with the de Montforts, although parts of them may have survived throughout the medieval period. Tong was owned by the Harcourts from c1250 to c1270 and then passed to the Pembrugges. In c1300 they built a new hall on a north-south axis immediately east of the former ditch in front of the inner bailey east wall, which had presumably been reduced to its foundations by then. The subsequent mansions at Tong all had their principal rooms laid out on this axis on the same site, although each had various outbuildings elsewhere. The manor passed in 1447 to the Vernon family of Haddon Hall in Derbyshire, and between 1500 and his death in 1515 Sir Henry Vernon built a new mansion at Tong. This in turn was largely or entirely rebuilt by the Pierrepoint family in the late 17th century after being damaged during the Civil War when a Royalist garrison was stationed in the castle. In 1765 nearly all the traces of the earlier buildings were swept away when yet another new mansion designed by Capability Brown in an unusual moorish style was built for George Durant. This in turn became a ruin after military occupation in the 1914-18 war. It was demolished in 1954 on the pretext that it was dangerous.

Very little was known of the nature of the medieval buildings at Tong until extensive excavations were carried out in the 1970s prior to the building of the M54 motorway. Remains of the medieval parts were minimal. The footings of the Durant mansion and the medieval outer bailey wall had to be removed for the motorway, together with an 18th century ice-house probably incorporating remains of a 13th century round tower at the northern junction of the inner and outer baileys. Most of the inner bailey site survives in a now overgrown state immediately south of the motorway. It has retaining walls up to 5m high built in the late 17th century when this part was landscaped for a garden. Within it are a 14th or 15th century well 12.5m deep and the footings of a kitchen thought to have been last used c1300. East of these is a remnant of what is supposed to have been a chapel on the basis of pieces of stained glass and tracery found in the excavations, and some cellars which lay below outbuildings of the 18th century mansion. Foundations of a smithy and stable and other offices of that period survive on the north side of the motorway, above the shore of the lake.

The motte and folly, Tutbury Castle

Tutbury *North of town, 5 miles north-west of Burton upon Trent.*

In 1071 William I gave Tutbury to Henry, Lord of Ferriers and Chambrais in Normandy. On a splendid defensive site above the River Dove he built a castle to serve as his principal residence and administrative centre for over two hundred manors. It comprised a large D-shaped bailey with a rampart and deep ditch which was approached originally by a natural gully between two equally spacious outer baileys on the east, and which is dominated by a motte at the west end. Robert de Ferrers, third son of Henry, was created Earl of Derby in 1138. The third Earl, William, joined the rebellion of Henry II's sons in consequence of which Tutbury Castle was besieged and captured by the King in 1174, and the timber buildings were dismantled the following year. Rebuilding in stone gradually followed. There are foundations of a chapel of c1190 in the bailey, and the shell keep which formerly crowned the motte was perhaps built about that time. In c1225-40 it was supplemented by a new round tower keep of which traces under the grass can be seen on the north-west side of the bailey.

Earl Robert de Ferrers supported Simon de Montfort against Henry III, and in 1263 Prince Edward laid waste the Earl's lands and damaged the castle. After de Montfort's defeat and death at Evesham in 1265 Tutbury was granted by Henry III to his younger son Edmund, created Earl of Lancaster in 1267. Either Edmund or his son Thomas built a new suite of apartments on the south side of the bailey. These survived until the end of the 16th century and comprised a hall over 18m long and a great chamber 14m long, both being nearly 9m wide. In 1313-4 Earl Thomas spent £100 on building the existing gatehouse, a rectangular tower 11m by 8m with a guard room on the south-east side of a wide passageway, with a single chamber on each storey above. Thomas led the baronial opposition to Edward II. He was defeated at Burton-on-Trent in 1322, and captured and executed later the same year. Tutbury Castle was plundered by the royal troops but most of the Earl's money was lost in the River Dove while being carted away and was not found again until the 19th century.

South Tower at Tutbury Castle

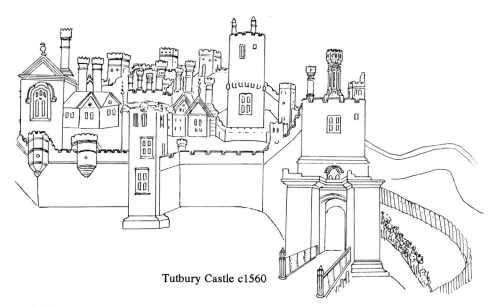

Tutbury Castle c1560

In 1326 Edward II returned Tutbury to Thomas's brother Henry, whose heiress Blanche married Edward III's third son John of Gaunt, then created Duke of Lancaster. The Duke was often in France, or at court, or at one of his many other castles, but Tutbury seems to have been frequently used by his wife. Repairs are recorded in 1362, and building was in progress in the 1390s. The Duchy of Lancaster was merged with the Crown in 1399 and has belonged to the sovereign ever since. A new tower, which has not survived, was being built during Henry IV's visits in 1404 and 1405, and work on a fresh section of curtain walling was begun prior to his death in 1413. Under his grandson Henry VI much of the present curtain wall, now reduced to its base, was erected. Work started at the southern end in 1420 and proceeded slowly until 1442, when the South Tower was begun. From 1446 to 1461 Tutbury was held by the Queen, Margaret of Anjou, for whom the North Tower was built in 1457-60. This is an ashlar-faced structure 10.6m by 9.6m with a vaulted basement almost buried in the earlier rampart and three storeys of fine rooms above, these being reached directly from the court by a spiral stair in a projecting turret. The South Tower has a western part similar in size and layout to the North Tower, and an eastern part of even greater size. It was probably intended to provide an extensive suite of private royal chambers and dominate the town below, and was designed to rise far above its present height of just two storeys.

The Yorkist and Tudor kings never used the castle and it was left to decay. The shell keep was ruined by 1500, the kitchen roof had fallen by 1516, and by 1523 many roofs were leaking and on the section of curtain wall between the gatehouse and the North Tower was a longitudinal crack. It was not until after Elizabeth I's accession in 1558 that repairs were begun. A somewhat fanciful sketch made around that time shows the castle as a magnificent structure with many towers and turrets and chimneys. It is particularly useful in that it shows the vanished round tower keep on the north-west side.

81

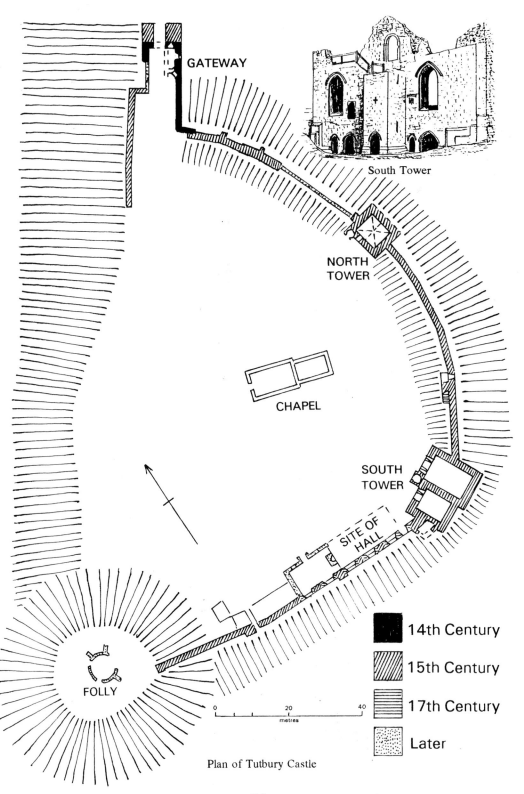

GATEWAY

South Tower

NORTH
TOWER

CHAPEL

SOUTH
TOWER

SITE OF
HALL

FOLLY

0   20   40
metres

■ 14th Century

▨ 15th Century

▤ 17th Century

▦ Later

Plan of Tutbury Castle

Mary, Queen of Scots was incarcerated at Tutbury in the care of the Earl of Shrewsbury during the first half of each of 1569 and 1570, the medieval hall and chamber being subdivided with wainscotted partitions to make what were then considered more suitable sized rooms. In 1585 she was again at Tutbury in the custody of Sir Ralph Sadler, Chancellor of the Duchy, who took her riding and hawking and tried to make her comfortable in a timber framed apartment block near the North Tower. However, Mary complained of the smell of a nearby privy without a drain and her lack of privacy, and things got worse when Sir Ralph was replaced Sir Amyas Paulet, a Puritan who was stricter with her and who occupied the gatehouse upper rooms. By the 1590s the gateway of the lower court was almost roofless and the North tower badly cracked. James I must have carried out repairs as he came several times to go hawking in Needwood Forest. Charles I stayed in 1634 and other years and had the medieval hall replaced by a new block for which large new windows were pierced through the curtain wall.

The castle withstood a short siege in 1643 and was visited by the King and Prince Rupert in 1645. It surrendered to Parliamentary forces after a three week siege in April 1646 and was slighted the next year. Some of the rooms were patched up in 1662 and leased to the Duke of Ormonde. From 1681 until 1864 the castle was leased to the Vernons who built a new house on the south side and built follies on the motte and South Tower. Excavations have shown that the inner part of the bailey rampart is not Norman but 18th century landscaping over the debris of the slighted curtain wall and the buildings which leaned against it. The house was later altered and extended and is still used by the resident caretaker. The Duchy has been admitting paying visitors to the ruins since 1847.

Old print of Tutbury Castle

Walsall *West of town centre.*

A shallow depression around a block of flats near a hospital is the last relic of the moat filled in during the 1970s. It was probably dug for Ralph, Lord Bisset in 1338, and there was an abortive attempt by Sir Ralph Bisset to build a new castle here in the 1380s, when 542 cartloads of stone were delivered. In 1388-9 a new drawbridge across the moat was provided and the wooden gates plated with iron. It passed to the Beauchamp Earls of Warwick in 1390 and was allowed to decay, the moat being leased as a fishery in 1438. The house had gone by 1576 and the northern arm of the moat was filled in during the 1870s.

Warwick *By the River Avon, immediately south of the town.*

When William I built a motte and bailey castle beside the River Avon at Warwick in 1068, four houses belonging to the Abbot of Coventry had to be destroyed, probably to provide a clear field of fire on the north side. Henry de Beaumont was installed as constable and after he was created Earl of Warwick by William II in 1088 the castle came to be regarded as his private property. Henry founded a church of All Saints in the castle but the Bishop of Worcester objected to its position within a private fortress and had it transferred c1127. The next Earl, Roger, supported King Stephen and is said to have died of chagrin in 1153 after the garrison at Warwick was tricked into surrendering the castle to the Empress Maud's son Henry of Anjou, who was crowned as Henry II in the following year.

The motte, Warwick Castle

The sheriff of Warwick had the wooden buildings on the motte rebuilt and provisioned during the rebellion of Henry II's sons in 1173. A mason named Ralph was employed to carry out repairs in 1191 so by then parts of the bailey palisade may already have been replaced by stone walls. King John had the castle garrisoned in 1205. Margery, heiress of the 6th Earl who died in 1242, married one of the Marshal family and the castle was surrendered to Henry III's officials during Richard Marshal's revolt of 1233 as there was no male heir to be handed over as a hostage instead. On the mound summit there remain the three sides facing the bailey of a polygonal shell keep, probably built in this period but remodelled and given new turrets and battlements in the 17th and 18th centuries. After her second husband died in 1263 the castle and earldom passed to Margery's cousin William Mauduit. In 1264 John Giffard made a surprise attack on Warwick, breached the wall, probably on the east side, and took the Earl off to Kenilworth where he was kept until a ransom of 1,900 marks was paid. This Earl was succeeded in 1268 by his nephew William Beauchamp.

William was the first of six Beauchamp Earls of Warwick who were leading warriors and courtiers and rebuilt the castle in a style in accordance with their power and influence. The second of them, Guy, held Edward II's despised favourite Piers Gaveston at Warwick in 1312 and executed him on Blacklowe Hill. The third Earl, Thomas, began in the 1340s a splendid new suite of apartments overlooking the river of which the extensive vaulted undercrofts remain. Ransoms from French nobles captured at the battle of Poitiers in 1356 are said to have helped pay for rebuilding the east side of the castle as a magnificent show front with a central gatehouse and barbican with polygonal turrets, and towers at either end. The trilobed Caesar's Tower of c1370-85 rises from a broad base through six storeys to a height of 44m above the river. The narrower top two storeys form a turret-like structure within the main machicolated parapet. According to Dugdale the 38m high Guy's Tower was completed in 1394 by the 4th Earl, another Thomas, who had been Governor to the young Richard II. It is a twelve sided structure containing four comfortable private apartments and also has a machicolated parapet. These works stand complete and little altered although the existing parapets appear to be mostly 17th and 18th century replacements.

Guy's Tower, Warwick Castle

Gatehouse, Warwick Castle

Old print of Warwick Castle from the River Avon

Henry, the 6th Beauchamp Earl of Warwick was elevated to a Dukedom in 1445 by Henry VI but died soon after leaving an infant daughter who died in 1449. The castle then passed to his sister Anne whose husband Richard Neville, heir of the Earl of Salisbury, was confirmed as Earl of Warwick. He was the famous "Warwick The Kingmaker" who firstly helped put Edward IV on the throne in 1461 but later became jealous of the latter's favourites and ended up briefly restoring Henry VI to power. After Earl Richard and his brother were killed at the Battle of Barnet in 1471 Edward IV granted the castle and earldom to his own brother George, Duke of Clarence who was executed in 1478 for treason. The Crown then administered the earldom until 1547 and shortly after his seizure of power in 1483 Richard III began building a huge rectangular tower with octagonal tower towers furnished with gunports in the middle of the weak north side. It is unlikely that this tower was completed above its present height of a single storey and the innermost portion of it was removed in the 18th century when the remainder was levelled off and embattled. However the creation in 1486 of the office of keeper of artillery at the castle (which has no other gunports) suggests that the tower was then furnished with cannon as intended.

Warwick Castle was handed over to John Dudley when he was created Earl of Warwick in 1547. Repairs were soon put in hand as the shell keep on the motte was very cracked, and 500 cartloads of stone from the recently dissolved Dominican Friary were required to underpin the south wall and prevent the domestic buildings falling into the river. A tiled roof from the friary had already been reused on a kitchen added by Henry VIII at the east end of the apartments. Earl John became Duke of Northumberland but was executed by Queen Mary after the abortive attempt in 1553 to crown Lady Jane Grey as Queen. Elizabeth I restored Ambrose Dudley to the earldom in 1558 and visited him at the castle in 1566 and again in 1572, when a new timber framed range on a stone basement was erected. When the Earl died childless in 1590 and the castle reverted to the Crown it was reported to be very decayed, mainly on account of lead having been stolen from the roofs of the domestic buildings.

In 1604 James I granted the castle to Sir Fulke Greville of Beauchamps' Court, a descendant of a minor branch of the Beauchamps. He spent more than £20,000 renovating the apartments and laying out the grounds. He was created Baron Brooke in 1621 and was succeeded by his cousin Robert who was killed whilst leading a Parliamentary storming force against Lichfield Cathedral Close in 1643. The castle had been fortified early in 1642 with cannon and outer earthworks, and under the command of Sir Edward Peyto had withstood a siege lasting a fortnight by royalist troops led by the Earl of Northampton. In 1645 there were over 300 troops in the castle. There were cannon mounted on the motte and perhaps also the flat roof of Guy's Tower.

Much repairwork and remodelling was carried out in the 1660s and 70s for the 4th Lord Brooke when the block outside the north-east curtain was added. The 8th Lord was created Earl Brooke in 1746 and Earl of Warwick in 1759, the castle and earldom having had separate holders since the death of Ambrose Dudley. This lord gothicised many of the windows in the apartments, refurnished many of the rooms, and added the dining room at the east end. In 1978 the then Lord Brooke sold the castle and what remained of its furnishings to Madame Tussauds who continue to maintain it as one of Britain's premier tourist attractions.

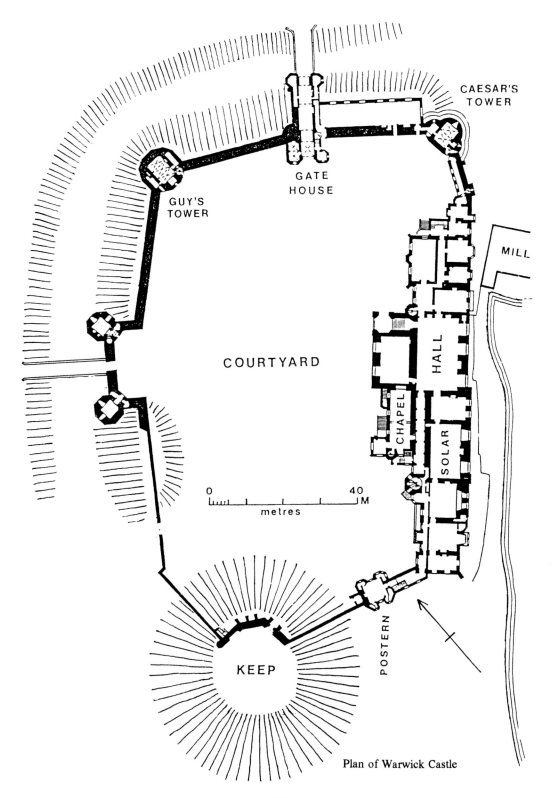

CAESAR'S TOWER

GATE HOUSE

GUY'S TOWER

COURTYARD

MILL

CHAPEL

HALL

SOLAR

0   40
                M
metres

KEEP

POSTERN

Plan of Warwick Castle

Weoley *South-west Birmingham suburb, near Selly Oak.*

The Paganels had an oval moated platform with timber buildings beside a stream here in the mid 12th century. It passed to Ralph de Somery who seems to have built a stone hall on the eastern part of the platform c1200. The present walls averaging 1.2m thick above a broad battered plinth rising directly from the bottom of the moat, and the consequent enlargement of the platform, probably date from soon after 1267 when Henry III licensed Roger de Somery to fortify the site. They enclose a rectangle 75m long by 60m wide with the south-west corner canted off, have thin pilaster buttresses at intervals and small square towers projecting beyond the middle of the north, south, and south-west sides, plus another at the north-east corner. A further tower projecting internally near the north-west corner contained the gateway passage, later blocked at the outer end. Later in this period a new stone hall was added with a kitchen at the south end, a solar at the north end, and a barn built somewhere on the west side.

After Sir John de Somery died in 1322 Weoley went to his sister Joan, married to Thomas Botetort. They and their successors added a second barn and built the chapel and the apartment block for guests against the north wall, and the garderobe complex in the north-east corner. The octagonal turret at the south-east corner is perhaps late 14th century, whilst the round turret near the gatehouse is probably still later. In 1384 the heiress Joyce de Botetort brought Weoley to Sir Hugh de Burnell, who held it until 1430. Weoley was held by the Berkeleys from 1439 until confiscated in 1485 by the newly crowned Henry VII and given to the Dudleys. They sold the castle to Richard Jerveys, Sheriff of London, in 1536, and his descendants held Weoley until the early 19th century although it was a ruin by the mid 17th century and took no part in the Civil War.

Weoley Castle

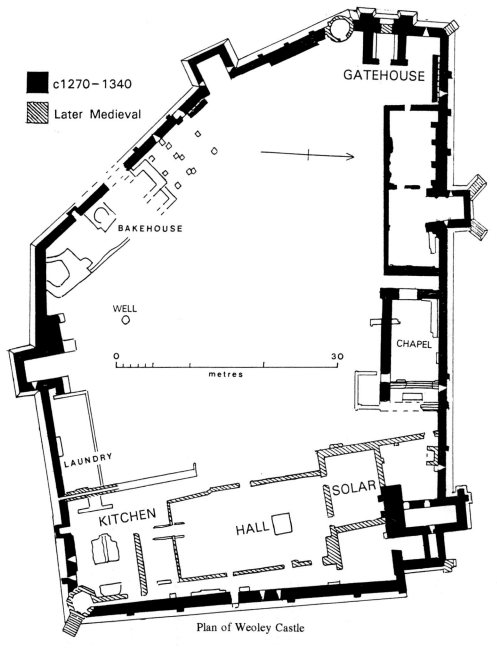

c1270–1340

Later Medieval

GATEHOUSE

BAKEHOUSE

WELL

0   30

metres

CHAPEL

LAUNDRY

SOLAR

KITCHEN

HALL

Plan of Weoley Castle

By the 20th century the walls and buildings had crumbled away almost down to courtyard level and were covered with silt and debris. A long series of excavations were begun in the 1930s, continuing up to 1962. Despite the loss of early excavation reports in a fire during World War II it was possible to reconstruct the mostly forgotten history of the site. A detailed description of the castle as it was in 1424 allowed the identification of most of the rooms. It is now maintained by Birmingham City Council and is open to the public.

Whichford   *10 miles west-south-west of Banbury.*

West of the village is a platform 60m square surrounded by a wet moat which on the east side is held in by an outer bank because of the fall of ground. This was the site of a castle built by the Mohun family in the early 14th century. It passed to Richard, Lord Strange in 1405, went to the Stanleys in the 16th century and was sold to the Sheldons in the early 17th century.

Whitacre   *At a farm 7 miles south of Tamworth.*

It was probably Ralph Basset of Drayton, to whom the manor was leased and then conveyed in 1320, who built the nearly square wet moat with a stone inner lining flanked at each corner except the north-east by a low square sandstone tower or bastion with a loop in each wall. On the south side is a tiny late 16th century gatehouse. Within the moat is an L-shaped house rebuilt in the 18th century except for the 17th century back wing. The manor later passed to the Birminghams, Whittacres, Ferrers, Chetwynds, Devereux, Longevilles, and Cheneys. In 1542 the house was leased to John Starkey.

Whitwick   *In village centre between Leicester and Derby.*

East of the church is a natural hill 100m long on top and 10m high on the south but higher on the other sides where there is a stream at the foot. There is a house at the north end and a small mound in the middle. The Earl of Leicester had a castle here by the 1140s, it being mentioned in the treaty he made in 1148 with the Earl of Chester. It passed to the Earl of Winchester and was destroyed in 1217 by the Earl of Pembroke. There are no remains of the house which Henry Beaumont was licensed to crenellate here in 1320 which later passed to the Hastings family.

Old print of Wolseley Castle

Wolseley   *In the Trent Valley between Rugeley and Stafford.*

In 1469 Edward IV licensed Ralph Wolseley to crenellate his house in the Trent Valley between Colwich and Rugeley. Considerable scattered ruins of various buildings are shown in a late 18th century engraving suggesting a possible layout like Wingfield Manor or Haddon Hall with courts either side of a central hall block. The present building on the site does not appear to be of anv great age. The pool to the west may be associated with a former moat. The Wolseley family have lived here from the 11th century until the present century.

Worcester   *Immediately south of the cathedral.*

A major row broke out in 1069 when Ealdred, Archbishop of York, formerly Bishop of Worcester, objected to Urse D'Abitot, Sheriff of Worcestershire, taking part of the cemetery of the cathedral-priory to build the outer defences of a new motte and bailey castle. The Beauchamp family, in which the office of sheriff became hereditary, held the castle throughout the 12th century. In 1113 the wooden buildings were destroyed by a fire that consumed much of the city. The motte, the wooden tower upon it, the gateway, bridge, bailey palisade, hall, chambers and the cellars of the King's houses within the castle are all mentioned in the sheriffs' accounts during the reigns of Henry II and Richard I. The expenditure was modest and was probably only refers to repairs. King John, who frequently visited Worcester and was buried in the Cathedral in 1216, ordered the sheriff in 1204 to rebuild the wooden gatehouse in stone, which was done for £40. In the last year of the reign the castle was held by William Marshal the younger and was besieged by a force loyal to the King under Ranulph de Blundeville, Earl of Chester, and Fawkes de Breaute.

Immediately after King John's death the monks of the cathedral-prior petitioned the young Henry III for the ground taken by Urse D'Abitot to be returned to them. The baileys were duly handed over whilst the motte and tower remained in the custody of Walter de Beauchamp. His seat was at Elmley and what was left of Worcester Castle was allowed to decay. It was presumably untenable in 1263 when Robert Ferrers, Earl of Derby, entered and sacked the city "through the old castle". The county prison stood on the site for many years until transferred to another site in 1809. A map of 1741 shows both the motte and the southern rampart of inner bailey still remaining. The motte rose 24m above the river. The last remains of it were finally removed in 1848.

A GLOSSARY OF TERMS

Ashlar — Masonry of blocks with even faces and square edges.

Bailey — An enclosure defended by walls, palisades, or moats.

Barbican — A porch, tower, or enclosure defending a gateway.

Bartizan — A turret corbelled out from a wall.

Bastion — A projection the same height as the main defensive line.

Battlement — A parapet with crenellations protecting a wall-walk.

Brattice — A wooden gallery with machicolations overhanging a wall.

Chancel — The eastern part of a church containing the main altar.

Corbel — A projecting bracket supporting stonework or timbers.

Crenellations — The indentations in a parapet.

Curtain Walls — High stone walls around a castle bailey.

Forebuilding — A fortified porch defending the entrance of a keep.

Four-centred — Drawn with the compass on four separate points.

Jamb — The side of a doorway, window, or other opening.

Keep — A building or small court forming the ultimate strongpoint.

Light — A compartment of a window.

Machicolation — Slots behind a parapet for dropping or firing missiles.

Merlons — The upstanding portions of a crenellated parapet.

Moat — A ditch around an enclosure. May be dry or water filled.

Motte — A steep sided mound, usually at least partly artificial.

Mullion — A vertical member dividing the lights of a window.

Nave — The part of a church or chapel used by the congregation.

Parapet — A wall for protection at any sudden drop.

Pilaster — A flat buttress. Common in the 12th and 13th centuries.

Piscina — A stone basin for washing out holy vessels after mass.

Plinth — The protecting base of a wall. Normally stepped or battered.

Portcullis — A wooden gate designed to rise and fall in vertical grooves.

Postern — A secondary gateway or back doorway.

Ringwork — A medium sized enclosure defended by a rampart and ditch.

Shell Keep — A small stone walled enclosure on top of a motte.

Solar — The lord's private living room, often also his bedroom.

Tower House — A tower forming a self contained military and domestic unit.

Transom — A horizontal member dividing top and bottom window lights.

Wall-walk — A walkway protected by a parapet on top of a curtain wall.

OTHER BOOKS BY MIKE SALTER

PUBLISHED BY FOLLY PUBLICATIONS
Folly Cottage, 151 West Malvern Rd, Malvern, Worcs, WR14 4AY

A   Castles & Moated Mansions of Shropshire 1988 (1992 reprint) 76 pages 94 illus.

B   Old Parish Churches of Shropshire 1988 (1992 reprint) 76 pages 109 illustrations

C   Castles & Moated Mansions of Staffordshire 1989 (1993 reprint) 64 pages 72 illus.

D   Old Parish Churches of Staffordshire 1989 76 pages 114 illustrations

E   Old Parish Churches of Worcestershire 1989 76 pages 144 illustrations.

F   Castles of Herefordshire and Worcestershire 1989 (1992 reprint) 68 pages 87 illus.

G   Old Parish Churches of Herefordshire 1990 (1993 reprint) 76 pages 112 illustrations

H   Parish Churches of The Forest of Dean 1990 40 pages 82 illustrations

J   Old Parish Churches of Gwent, Glamorgan & Gower 1991 76 pages 177 illus.

K   Castles of Gwent, Glamorgan & Gower 1991 76 pages 123 illustrations

L   Castles of Mid Wales 1991 56 pages 90 illustrations

M   Old Parish Churches of Mid Wales 1991 56 pages 123 illustrations

N   Castles & Moated Mansions of Warwickshire 1992 56 pages 87 illustrations

O   Old Parish Churches of Warwickshire 1992 72 pages 170 illustrations

P   Old Parish Churches of North Wales 1993 72 pages 192 illustrations

Q   Castles and Stronghouses of Ireland 1993 160 pages 471 illustrations

R   Castles of South-West Scotland 1993 152 pages over 300 illustrations

S   Old Parish Churches of Scotland 1994 120 pages about 300 illustrations

T   Old Parish Churches of South-West Wales 1994 No details yet available

1994 prices: Q,R,S £7.50 C,J,K,P £3.95 A,B,D,F,G,H,L,M,N,O £3.00
Postage & packing £1 Irish & Scottish titles, 50p English & Welsh titles.
A minumum charge of £10 is made for single book orders from retail shops.

QuercuS

… publisning interesting books …

Quercus is a regional publisher specialising in books about Wales and the western Midlands. We are interested in the region yesterday, today and tomorrow; in landscapes and language, trees meadows and flowers, history, battles, lords and kings, castles and churches, bridges and tunnels. We want to know about industries and towns, people and customs, parks and playgrounds, myths and hauntings. In fact we are interested in anything that interests you.

"The Trackway of the Cross" was the first Quercus title, about a path across North Wales trodden by 6th century Irish monks. It was followed by "Sketches of Hales Owen", forty pen an ink drawings by a local artist with commentary.

Future titles include "Australian Williams". William Williams of Anglesey worked his passage to Australia, dug for gold, found it, and came home to found a building firm in Liverpool. He taught himself to read and write in English and Welsh and the story is based on his diaries.

Soon we hope to issue "Midland Woods & Forests" "Midland Rivers & Streams", "Midland Lakes & Ponds", "Haunted Buildings in the Midlands" and "Midland Parks".

We are always willing to discuss ideas and proposals for new titles. If you have an idea but do not think you are up to writing about it, talk to us anyway. John Roberts might suggest coauthorship with you providing the research.

8 Hillside Close, Bartley Green, Birmingham
B32 4LT   021 550 3158